The Adventures of a Bush Pilot

Library of Congress Catalogue Number
70-522-6067(L)

International Standard Book Number:
0-9658373-0-0

This work is nonfiction
For information address; Richard H. LaPorte
RR 2, Box 128C, Newport, NH 03773

Second printing l999

CONTENTS

CONTENTS

DEDICATION

I dedicate this book in memory of my mother and father, Grace & Reginald LaPorte, and to my lovely wife, Joyce. Also, let me not forget all my friends that have flown with me throughout the years. Lastly, I wish to give thanks to my brother Wayne LaPorte and his wife Judy for the use of their dock on Lake Sunapee to park my seaplane for so many years.

INTRODUCTION

While sitting back, relaxing in the comforts of a recliner, how often I have thought how interesting and entertaining it would be to recap some of those special moments in life. Be it comical, death threatening, or some wild and challenging experience. My life has been full of adventure and hair raising experiences far beyond the point of believing. When telling my stories to groups or individuals, I often get accused of stretching the truth. I have been asked many times, "How could it be?" My answer to that is, "Because it happened to me." Perhaps that question would not have been asked if they had lived the experiences as I did.

In writing this book, I briefly highlight my years as a young boy developing into a certain kind of character. This may help one understand what motivated me for the years to come as to my hobbies and professions. Perhaps, it might best be said, there was a great aspiration to do things others around me would- n't dream of. It was like I was being driven by some kind of force accompanied by a certain design of discipline. As though my destiny had been previously written.

INTRODUCTION

Because of the many fascinating, thrilling and hair raising experiences in my life as a bold and daring bush pilot and guide, I felt compelled to write this book. It is a collection of short stories covering a period of more than fifty years.

Flying sportsmen on hunting and fishing trips into northern Quebec was only a tiny portion of what began as my childhood fantasies. It kept my interests for more than a quarter of a century. An extension of my flying north includes a story about my wild and exciting seaplane trip to Alaska.

It is about hunting trophy caribou in the far reaches of the north country. Of being charged by the giant bull moose, to pursuing the beautiful speckled brook trout of trophy size.

There are many dangers that accompany flying in the north country. At times, with a blink of an eye, wicked, fierce storms would sweep in on us, carrying big winds, snow, or rain and fog. This can be a pilot's worst nightmare. We have a saying, "if you are in a hurry, don't fly." These are true and living experiences I share with those who read this book.

WHEN
I WAS YOUNG

To give a better understanding of my character and the kind of life I led, I begin by writing about my early days. The molding of my life that brought me to my greatest enjoyment and final profession as a bush pilot. My destiny and dream come true.

I was born on December 22, 1932 in Barre, Vermont during an old fashion winter blizzard, back when times were tough and my parents were struggling to afford a quart of milk. The depression made life very difficult. My father, a quiet, easy going man of French descent was a mechanic struggling to make a living in a small garage business. My mother was of English descent, with dark hair and of medium stature, stayed busy caring for the home, taking care of us kids and helping my father whenever possible.

When I was approximately two years old, the family moved to North Newport, New Hampshire. It was a small settlement with only a few houses scattered about the countryside. A place where people enjoyed their lives in peace.

WHEN I WAS YOUNG

It wasn't long before a certain life style started to take shape. When I was about the age of six, our family adopted a newfoundland dog from a family who found his size so overwhelming, they could no longer care for him. He was so big, I, my brothers Wayne and Junior, and sisters Vivian, Tootie and Margaret, thought the only appropriate name for him was "Tiny". He had long, shiny black hair, huge paws, and a large head with a powerful set of jaws, seemingly, always dripping with drool. He was a great dog for us kids.

Occasionally, as my mother was preparing to bake and when there wasn't a watchful eye around, Tiny's favorite thing to do, was to sneak a pound or two of butter, or lard from the kitchen shelf. All of us kids decided we had better try something to break him of the habit, or our parents might get rid of our dog. We figured, just maybe, a liberal amount of mom's cayenne pepper applied to a pound of lard would do the trick. Sure enough, a short time later, Tiny was running for the closest bucket of water. He was breathing fire like it was coming from a stoked up locomotive, and his eyes were so bloodshot, he could hardly see. It was only after that, the thievery slow down.

I often think about the local swimming hole in a small brook at the edge of the village. It seemed, Tiny could never let us kids go there without coming along. For one reason, or another, whenever I jumped into the pool for a swim, our giant one hundred and sixty five pound newfoundland thought he had to rescue me. He continually insisted on dashing into the pool, grab me by the trunks and haul me out of the water. I know he had particularly taken a shine to me. It may

WHEN I WAS YOUNG

have been because I spent so much time with him. He came to be such a nuisance, When we had intentions of doing much swimming, we had to leave him home.

Winter was upon us, and with a fresh snowfall, my dad and I were off to do a little rabbit hunting. We didn't have a beagle dog, so we decided to take Tiny, our prize newfoundland with us. While back in the woods, and standing a short distance from my dad, I could hear the excitement in Tiny's barking. Hopefully, he was hot on the trail of a rabbit. All of a sudden, and much to my surprise, a rabbit came hopping along and dove between my legs.

It didn't take much snow to come high up on my legs those days, being how short and small I was. Tiny wasn't paying any attention to where he was going, or who was standing where. He was right on the heels of the rabbit with his nose tight to the ground sniffing the fresh scent of the rabbit tracks leading straight between my legs. The next thing I knew, I was bowled end over end by our giant rabbit dog. Tiny was so excited with this new experience, he failed to see me standing there. Maybe he thought he could fit between my legs like the rabbit did. Perhaps if he had been a small beagle, I may not have been so sore for the next week or two. There has been a few times when I wished I were taller.

Still at an early age, I decided to fit our prize newfoundland sled dog to a harness and have a sled dog to pull me around town. Well, you may have guessed it, something had to go wrong. While driving my newly discovered sled dog down the road leading through

WHEN I WAS YOUNG

the village, several stray dogs off in a pine grove, raised a ruckus when they spotted Tiny.

Through the snow bank we went, gaining speed with Tiny's every leap, with the sled totally out of control. Dodging the trees was next to impossible. The sled ricocheted from tree to tree, knocking bark off with each contact. I was hanging on for dear life, trying to bring my big dog to a halt, but nothing seemed to work. I was at the mercy of whatever was to happen.

With Tiny in full chase, he all of a sudden made a swerve around a two foot pine tree. The sled came to a crashing halt and left me straddling the tree. Understandably, being sore and not walking well, it brought an early end to my dog sledding days. It seems as though my pet dog Tiny had caused me one pain too many.

As time passed and I reached nine years of age, a friend gave me an old octagon barreled twenty-two caliber rifle. Though it was missing a firing pin and being an old relic that had been laying around for years, I became quite proud of owning my first rifle. Of course, everyone figured as long as the firing pin was missing, it was considered safe. After all, how could a nine year old have the intuition to get it to work.

It wasn't long before I discovered how to dismantle the rifle that an idea struck me. I nailed the rifle barrel to the back window sill of our old outhouse and slid a bullet into the chamber. One stroke of a nail hammer on the end of the shell fired a bullet into a target set against a large pine tree at the foot of the bank.

When that got to be old stuff, I reassembled the rifle and started looking into how I could fix it to shoot like it was made to. I soon learned, that by cutting a certain size finish nail to the proper length, it worked just fine for a firing pin. I had to be careful not to tip the butt end of the gun towards the ground for fear the firing pin might fall out.

We were a hunting family. My dad had gone up north deer hunting for the day. I figured this gave me and my younger brother Wayne, and sister Tootie a chance to go hunting on our own locally. With a supply of home made firing pins tucked away in my shirt pocket, we struck out over the hills in search of squirrels and other small game.

A short time later, we came upon a logging road. There sat the prettiest red fox we had ever seen. We studied the animal for several minutes before deciding for sure it wasn't our neighbor's german shepherd. As I took steady aim, my eyes glanced at an empty firing pin slot. Somehow, the firing pin had managed to fall out. I reached into an empty pocket, discovering I had also lost the spare firing pins.

Some fast thinking told me to go back to a barbed wire fence we had crossed earlier. With luck, I could break off a barb with two stones. Just maybe, it would work in place of a finish nail.

My brother and sister stayed behind to keep an eye on the fox while I worked feverishly on getting the barb off the fence. Much to my surprise, it fit perfectly.

I made my way back, happy to see the fox still sitting on the stump. I raised the rifle slowly and took

WHEN I WAS YOUNG

steady aim and fired. After the first shot broke its back, the fox was running around in circles, I was forced to use my last two bullets on him. When they failed to kill him, I had to use several clubs to do him in, but only after he had put his teeth through the toe of my leather boots. We then strung the fox to a pole and proudly carried it native style to our home to hang where my dad hangs his deer in the shed.

Upon his return, our dad was surprised to see our big accomplishment, but after hearing about our little episode, he restricted the use of the rifle. For awhile, our hunting days were slightly curtailed whenever dad was away.

Growing up during my school days was tough enough, but being short of pocket money was worse. A bounty of fifty cents to a dollar for each porcupine killed was paid by the town. In some cases, either the nose or head had to be shown to the selectmen before collecting the money.

Nights after school, I would head for the mountain with my flashlight and club to do some bounty hunting. Some nights, I got as many as sixteen porcupines. The next day I would arrive at the selectmen's office to collect my bounty. It got so, the selectmen preferred not to look into the bag containing noses or heads because of the stench and decided to take my word as to how many there were.

For a few years, I spent most of my time playing mountain man, ridding the forests and private domains of these pests. They stripped the bark off trees, chewed the tires of vehicles, and have been known to chew the brake hoses of vehicles thought to be park-

WHEN I WAS YOUNG

ed safely in their driveway. I would camp out high on the mountain laying quietly in wait for the slightest grunting or squealing noise of a porcupine as it made its way along a trail, jump up and rap it on the head with a club.

One time in particular, I remember seeing a porcupine in the top of a large maple tree. Climbing the tree was difficult enough, but I didn't think I was going to be outsmarted. The farther out on the limb I went, the farther out the porcupine would go until it was to the point of no return. It was getting toward evening and I had put so much effort into getting this critter, I didn't really want to give up. Maybe the lack of time pressured me into doing something I shouldn't have. I used to think if I grabbed the porcupine by the tail just right by sloping the quills backwards, I would not wind up with a fist full of quills. It was soon learned, that was a foolish thought. I spent the next hour pulling quills out of my hand. The porcupine won this round, so I wished him luck and headed home. I would deal with him later.

There was another occasion when they got me good, only in a different way. Porcupines had climbed upon my shoveldozer and chewed through several hydraulic lines. The following morning, as I began to operate the shoveldozer, there was a sudden shower of hot oil spraying from a high pressure hose. It was like I was sitting under a geyser. So much for that.

The day arrived when I finally got my first snowmobile. I would strap my pistol to my side and patrol the abandoned railroad bed, as well as the local logging roads. My feelings were changed over night. I

13

WHEN I WAS YOUNG

had become like a bounty hunter in a wild west movie with his pistol strapped to his side riding a bronco and chasing down outlaws. Only in this case, I was chasing down porcupines riding a snowmobile. When I came to a porcupine crossing the road in front of me, I would broad slide up to it, whip out my pistol and claim another bounty.

Throughout my school days, I spent my free time visiting old abandoned camps, caves, and stands of spruce or hemlock trees to help weed out the pesky porcupines. I must say, I still have several noses that are slightly dried from years past, waiting for the bounty to be put back on. Being forty years keeping them in my tool box drawer, they should be considered antique and perhaps a collector's item.

Throughout my younger years, and with all the things I got to doing, my interest in flying had been kicking around in the back of my mind. It was in the form of building model airplanes, flying kites, and watching how birds flew. Even at my young age, I was always thinking or dreaming how I could design my own airplane. I even went so far as to put a motor with a propeller on a sled to drive around the frozen lake with. The thought of putting wings on the sled came to me, but it never materialized. One day, the local newspaper reporter had to jump clear of the sled as he stood there taking pictures. As you may guess, I got out of control. Somewhere down the road, and unknown to me at the time, there was going to be a flying career for me. One thing stood in my mind. "If it was meant to be, I would fly. I just had to wait for that day."

SKIING THE DICK DURRANCE TRAIL

The one time famous Dick Durrance Ski trail located on the eastern face of Sunapee Mountain in Newbury, NH, had hosted some of the finest skiers around. It had been abandoned back in the nineteen forties with the exception of a few youngsters and die-hards that dare brave its narrow, twisty, dangerous, and unforgiving run from the top of the mountain.

There were sections of the trail near the top of the mountain so steep, when skiing down them, I had the feeling of losing my stomach. In other sections, there were large boulders requiring some quick action in maneuvering to avoid them.

One place in particular, a huge boulder lay at the crest of a steep hill. During a race, a skier forgot to go around it. He skied over the boulder, sailing through the air like he had come off a ski jump, only to get rapped around a beech tree about twenty feet up, breaking almost every bone in his body. I have known other skiers to make similar mistakes on other parts of the trail and meet similar disaster.

SKIING THE DICK DURRANCE TRAIL

There were no lifts available to transport the skiers up the mountain in the old days. Those that could afford seal skins, strapped them on their skis to aid in climbing the mountain.

While skiing the Dick Durrance Trail as a young boy, I had built a small jump at the top of the very last steep near the bottom of the mountain. It seemed that one of the professional skiers had lost control coming over the jump, for he wound up in a heap at the bottom of the hill with a broken leg. All I could hear was, "who built that jump?" My friends and I thought that was quite a joke. We were under the impression that a good skier should be able to handle himself under any condition. After that, the jump was quietly removed.

Towards spring, a flash flood had washed out the bridge at the bottom of the same steep where the jump was built. The bridge was about twenty feet wide where it spanned the brook. By now, the Ski Club had abandoned the trail for good, leaving it exclusively to us kids. Meaning two or three neighbors, my brother Wayne, and myself. I always said, if it wasn't for me, no one would have any thrills. It seemed I had to be the one to initiate all the ideas. Well, I had the crazy notion to build a jump on the mountain side of the brook, figuring that would allow us to ski the trail. We would be able to jump the brook and ski the last few hundred feet to the end.

The bed of the brook was full of rocks, leaving no room for mistakes. Because it was my idea, it was suggested by my young friends that I go first over the jump. The jump angled sharply up towards the sky

SKIING THE DICK DURRANCE TRAIL

and without having a previous trial run, it was anyone's guess as to how things would turn out. I always figured I could meet most challenges, even at my young age.

From the top of the hill, I let her rip. I needed all the speed I could get to make sure I would clear the brook. As I approached the jump at the bottom of the hill, my friends stood there cheering me on. The last I remembered when leaving the jump, I was looking straight up at clear, blue sky. I guess we hadn't properly calculated the angle of the jump. Luckily, I ended up on the other side of the brook. If I had been older, I would have called it embarrassing. I landed on my rear and got buried in the deep packed snow with my legs and skis sticking straight up in the air. That ended the final days of skiing the Dick Durrance Ski Trail.

ALMOST
FROZEN TO DEATH

At the age of thirteen, I had already become a big time deer hunter, having spent a lot of time in the woods and hunted with my father and friends. As time went on, our family enjoyed more time deer hunting in the Rangely Lakes area in the western part of the state of Maine.

We always liked to scout out new territory, looking for where the big bucks hang out. We eventually found ourselves on an old logging road leading in to Parmachenee Lake. The weather had turned miserable that day. It was raining, cold and foggy, dampening our spirits somewhat. But the family was well used to hunting in these conditions. It was Thanksgiving and we were on vacation. We had parked next to a cedar swamp hoping to spend a few hours hunting. Back in the old days before the cedar swamps were logged off, they gave me and my family some of our best hunting.

As I walked the deer trails that crisscrossed the thick green carpet of moss throughout the big cedar

ALMOST FROZEN TO DEATH

swamps, I would get a special kind of feeling. Especially, when I came upon big scrape marks on trees where a big buck had rubbed his horns, or saw big hoof prints in a pawed up bare spot on the deer trail. It may have been even a fresh pile of huge size droppings still steaming, indicating a big buck had just come through.

I usually sensed the presence of a big buck coming down a trail headed my way. At times, on a cold, frosty morning, a big buck would come running within a short distance of me, blowing and stomping the ground, kicking up quite a ruckus. The sound echoed throughout the forest in the stillness of the crisp, cool air. I would make a similar sound and stomp the ground with my boots to challenge him. The next thing I knew, he would come on the dead run directly towards me. Of course, that was a fatal mistake on his part, if he was a better than trophy size buck. Perhaps he was chasing the scent of a doe in heat.

Many times I have seen a big buck lurking in the shadows feeding on moss, or when I came onto a small clump of alders, or red berries. Maybe the big bucks had those particular places picked out for their lunch stops. I would try to remember where they were for the next time I would hunt there. It just seemed to happen that way so many times.

Unknown to me at the time, trouble started the moment my father checked his compass and I heard him mention the logging road ran north and south.

Why I failed to check my own compass, I will never know to this day. But somehow, I mistakenly assumed, that north was in the opposite direction of

ALMOST FROZEN TO DEATH

what it truly was.

The rain and fog persisted throughout the day as each of us was doing our own thing, poking our way through the woods, looking for the big, hard to get bucks. About the time I should have headed for the car, there was confusion. My sense of direction told me to go east to the car, but because I hadn't checked my own compass back at the road to verify my thinking on the direction of north, I was now in doubt. My father had always drummed into my head, never doubt my compass. So..., against my better judgment, I struck out in completely the opposite direction of the car, following my compass faithfully, not realizing how wrong I was to be.

All day long, I trudged steadily, crossing three rivers, and over territory I had never seen. I was seeing all kinds of wildlife and deer, not daring to shoot a single one, when finally, I came to a pond. By now, darkness had set in. My clothes were dripping wet, and my legs weary, as I groped my way through the woods. Sometimes, I stumbled over fallen trees or rocks, or ran face first into low hanging branches, while hoping to find a cabin, or road along the shore.

A river flowing out of the south end of the pond stopped me from going any further. I was forced to turn back, to make my way in pitch black around the north end of the pond.

Realizing it was hopeless to continue in the dark, there was little choice, but to make a shelter for the night using a spruce tree top and bows. Unknown to me at the time, a few hundred yards from where I made a place to stay, was a log cabin belonging to

ALMOST FROZEN TO DEATH

some old trapper. This was discovered in later years when returning to this area.

The temperature had dropped sharply during the night, falling to about zero degrees. Though I was soaked to the hide and had dry matches, I was too tired to bother building a fire. Wet, hungry and bewildered, I lay on the spruce bows I had prepared. To help keep warm, I drew my knees up close to my chin and pulled my hunting shirt over my head. I would draw in cold air and blow warm air from my breath to circulate under my shirt. When this process stopped working, my body began to shiver worse, and the colder I got.

The moment came, when I began to feel warm and comfortable. All the shaking and shivering had left me. I was at the point of freezing to death and was not aware of it. All senses seem to have left me. I attempted to straighten my legs to get more comfortable. It was then, when wicked, painful cramps set in my legs. They were so excruciating, the pain kept me from falling asleep, and more than likely, sure death.

It had been one of the longest nights of my life. At one point during the night, I was certain I heard rifle shots far away, signaling to me. My father and other "would-be" rescuers had gone deep into the woods that night attempting to locate me, firing their guns, but to no avail. I fired shots in response, but they were no doubt drowned out and carried away by the north wind.

Throughout the night, in his curiosity, a big buck was constantly blowing at me. I could tell it was a

ALMOST FROZEN TO DEATH

large buck because of the deep and powerful tone to its whistle like blowing, echoing in the cold, still of the night. I built the shelter beside a deer trail leading down to the pond and figured he must have been curious who was invading his territory. I told myself, "if you stay around until morning, I will at least have some delicious deer steak to eat."

During that longest night of my life, I had plenty of time to think about what went wrong, as to what got me into this predicament. Thoughts of the sun rising in back of the camp where we were staying, and the direction we drove to where we went into the woods, flashed through my mind. Then, everything began to fall in place. It was quite evident I had traveled in the opposite direction. If only I had checked my own compass back at the car, this would never have happened. I had to go east to get out.

Morning had finally come. I rubbed my aching legs and numb body to get some kind of circulation going. It was like bringing a half dead body back to life. I managed to hobble to my feet, happy to have survived the night to gaze through the cold, frosty, early dawn. I could see nothing but a sheet of ice suspended from the floor of the forest. I knew I had a long trip ahead of me, and didn't feel as though I could stay around to enjoy the beautiful sight of all the birch and poplar trees coated with ice crystals glistening in the sun's rays of the early morn. The pond had frozen over with about three inches of ice, reflecting how cold it had gotten that night.

With each step I took, it was echoed throughout the valley in the crisp, cold, frosty morning air. A second later, the air was filled with the shrill blowing sound of a big buck, "Shhhhu," the same buck that kept me company all night. His curiosity must have kept him browsing by the shore of the pond. My blood rushed through my body, sending a warm feeling of excitement all over me. He ran a short distance, to stop and wonder just who his visitor was.

As I waited nervously to get a glimpse of him, I noticed a branch like movement in a small opening by a stand of birches. The next instant, the gray face of the old buck appeared in full view with one of the biggest set of antlers I have ever seen. I eased my model 94 Winchester 30-30 slowly to my shoulder so as not to scare him, zeroed in on the white spot under his chin and fired. A thundering crash occurred, and then, dead silence.

After hesitating for a few moments, I made my way slowly to the opening to find the huge buck laying dead. Its antlers were massive, measuring thirty inches across its beam. Their bases were very heavy, and surrounded by many knobs jutting out. It was a trophy buck to be sure. One of the largest I have ever shot to date. I quickly dressed it, and propped it open with a stick between the rib cage to keep it from spoiling, then blazed the trees around it with my knife.

Soon, I was on a steady dog trot in the direction of the sun peeping over the hills. For four hours, I kept a steady pace, crossing the same three rivers I had crossed the day before. Only this time, I wasn't interested in looking for animals, I was anxious to get out to the dirt road and find my father. This time, my compass didn't let me down, for I finally came to the road where a Game Warden was waiting. In a matter of minutes, I was joined by my father, who was an emotional wreck. Tears streamed from his eyes as he put his arms around me to give me a big fatherly hug, happy to see me safe and sound.

It was Thanksgiving day, and being hungry for not having much to eat for a day and a half, I polished off a big chunk of turkey and half an apple pie that we had in the trunk of the car. On the way back to camp, we discussed the events of the past twenty four hours and the possibility of getting the big buck out of the woods.

This was a lesson to other sportsmen who may find them selves in a similar situation. Since this episode, I have spent many endless hours rescuing hunters from almost certain disaster.

MY EARLY
MANHOOD DAYS

After graduating from High School, I worked on construction for the state of New Hampshire, building a new highway. Six months later, I had joined the U.S. Air Force, taking me away from home for a period of four years. Three of those years were spent in England. To keep myself occupied, I joined the Air Force swimming team and competed in Germany in the United States Armed Forces in Europe swimming championships. While in England, I also competed in the United Kingdom swimming championships. Then, I was asked to join the U.S. Air Force Ski Team representing the United Kingdom, which I gladly accepted. I was part of a six member team that went to Garmisch, Germany to compete in the USAFE Skiing Championships in nineteen fifty three.

I guess I needed a little more excitement in my life, so I joined the local motorcycle club to compete in some of there events. I ordered a BSA Gold Star road racer through the base Post Exchange to be delivered to the local motorcycle dealer in Chester, England. Between racing in some of the local road races and becoming the first American to race in the

MY EARLY MANHOOD DAYS

Manx Grand Prix in the Isle of Man, my new venture brought me some unexpected trouble.

My commanding officer had given me an order not to do any more motorcycle racing. I had already entered the Grand Prix in the Isle of Man, and felt there was no way I was going to pass this one up. I was not aware of the stupid Air Force regulation stating that a G I will not participate in any sport that is considered hazardous. Of course, I would ask, "what sport is considered hazardous, and to whom?"

I attempted to conceal my identity as a U.S. serviceman when entering the race, but after the first day of racing, the cat was let out of the bag, so to speak. It appeared, when the press got a hold of the fact I was the first American to have ridden in the Grand Prix, they were on the phone to my commanding officer gathering what information about me they could. My name, as well as a picture of me standing beside my racing motorcycle in the paddock was plastered all over the front page of the newspapers. The news was also broadcast over the BBC (British Broadcasting) radio station.

A special meeting had to be held by the powers to be, the "Federation of International Motorcycling" and local Isle of Manx governing racing association to determine whether they should allow me to race the senior event the following day. I was not allowed to attend the meeting, but sat in the hallway just outside the meeting room nervously awaiting their decision. To my pleasure, they agreed to let me race.

I had a successful race and returned to my base, only to face a disciplinary board with the threat of all

MY EARLY MANHOOD DAYS

sorts of punishment. The officers at the hearing asked me what I had to say for my actions. I told them what I had accomplished in the last two years towards Anglo American relationships by joining in their sports was perhaps more than they had accomplished in the last ten years. That I saw no reason why servicemen could not be given approval to compete as I did. Well, I guess I took them by surprise, because they ended up taking only one stripe from me, telling me I could get it back when I hit state side. It was not long after, servicemen were allowed to race. Maybe my efforts hadn't been a total loss after all.

One year later, and back to civilian status, I became involved in my father's garage business. It wasn't until a few years after my father passed away that I was able to pursue my dream of becoming a bush-pilot.

THE
BEGINNING
OF A BUSH PILOT

Have you ever come to a point in your life when you have done almost everything but that one thing that hangs in the back of your mind, something special that you have always wanted to do, or become? "Yes," that day had finally come for me. My dreams and thoughts over the past years of becoming a bush pilot had finally come together.

As far as my priorities were concerned, years in the garage business, other interests, along with my professional motorcycle road racing and snowmobile racing got put to the bottom of my list. Regretfully, unknown to me at the time, my wife was to fall into that same list. She was elected to help run the business in my absence. My every day thoughts of becoming a bush pilot dominated everything I did. It became a powerful, wanting desire, like some compelling force within, driving me like I was destined for this new adventure.

THE BEGINNING OF A BUSH PILOT

It was the first day of August in the late nineteen sixties. Monday morning at the garage, I was trying my best to concentrate on my work, but found it most difficult. The young man working for me had just poked his head out from under the hood of a vehicle as I glanced up at the old round clock hanging on the wall. There was enough time. I laid my wrenches on the work bench and told my mechanic, "Take over, I'm headed for the airport."

Arriving at the airport with great anticipation, I strolled into a large hangar to inquire about flying lessons. One of the local pilots standing nearby told me to check with "Nick" the stocky built person working on an airplane. I was soon to find out, that this guy "Nick" was the manager of the Claremont Airport, mechanic, and also flight instructor. If you ever had any dealings with a Polish instructor, you may very well relate to my experience you are about to read.

After a brief introduction, I had convinced Nick to leave his work for the moment and give me my first flying lesson. He pointed out a small two place Cessna 150 parked next to a row of other aircraft and told me to check it over, he would be out shortly. I did not want to appear dumb about things, so put on like I knew what I was doing. Checking control surfaces, fuel drains, oil, and of course, fuel tanks and tires. A few minutes later, I was sitting behind the controls in the pilot's seat, with my Polish instructor beside me explaining a few necessary facts of flying the Cessna 150.

While taxiing to the end of the runway, I gradually got a better feel of the aircraft and tried to remember

THE BEGINNING OF A BUSH PILOT

the location of the instruments and their purpose. Nick muttered something in a low tone, which sounded like he was telling me to go ahead and show him what I knew about flying. I had already gotten a sense there was going to be a problem with communication.

After a quick runup and a check of the magnetos, I pointed the nose of the airplane down the runway. With my first lesson underway, I pushed the throttle to the dash and proceeded down the runway, vibrations and all. After a few bounces and a slight holding back on the controls, I experienced my first takeoff. As we climbed higher and higher, I looked below to see the runway getting smaller and further away. It was an exhilarating feeling, but my next thought, was how to land. Nick would mutter a few words, of which I heard little, but after flying around getting used to the airplane, I was soon enjoying takeoffs and landings.

I persistently stuck to flying at half hour segments, giving me enough time in between to absorb what I was suppose to be learning. I never could get much information from Nick, but a few grunts once and a-while. I resorted to asking other pilots that hung around the airport, but to my surprise, found very little help there. They were mostly weekend pilots, or what I now call fair weather pilots. They had either forgotten what they had learned, or just didn't know. So.., as it turned out, I studied the books and picked up a little information here and there, practically teaching myself what I had to know.

Needless to say, I did not spend much time at the garage that first week. My mind was totally on flying and getting my license. Thursday, was a nice day to

THE BEGINNING OF A BUSH PILOT

spend at the airport, so off I went. Nick told me to check out the Cessna 150 like he usually did. He climbed in on the copilot side and up we went. After flying the flight pattern around the airport and doing a few lazy eights, I was instructed to land the airplane and pull over to the side of the runway. Knowing the difficulty in communicating with Nick, I did not know what to expect. I only had about six hours and ten minutes of flying time, hardly enough to solo. Nick asks the big question. "Do you think you can fly this thing?" I swallowed hard, and before he had a chance to reconsider his offer, I answered with, "I don't see why not."

As Nick opened the cockpit door to step out, I felt a sudden rush of blood and warm sensation throughout my body. The big day had come. This was much quicker than most student pilots solo. Most instructors won't solo their students until after they have flown twenty to thirty hours.

Flying was definitely in my blood, and I knew that what I had in mind to do down the line, it wasn't going to stop here, just flying a Cessna 150.

It was in August when I first started ignoring my work at the garage to spend time flying. By September, and twenty five hours flying time later, my newly found flying friends and I were busy looking for a Cessna 206. It is one of Cessna's work horse. A six place airplane, with cargo doors and a powerful six cylinder, two hundred and eighty five horsepower engine. Nick had located a low time Cessna 206 over at Glens Falls, New York and thought we should take a look at it. The owner only liked flying on clear days.

THE BEGINNING OF A BUSH PILOT

Money was the biggest problem. Where could I come up with enough money before someone else jumped in and bought it out from under me. They say, "where there is a will, there is a way," because that was the case. I had to hock my motorcycle to give the owner five hundred dollars deposit to hold the airplane for one week.

Getting the big bucks to pay the balance was a headache. It was disappointing after approaching the president of the bank that held the mortgage on my property. He only laughed at me. I checked with two other banks I had done business with and got the same response. They all said the same thing. We have never financed an airplane before. Though I tried to convince them this was a good time to start, they would not listen to me.

Money was tight those days. I never had much free operating capital. Fortunately, a customer friend of mine heard of my predicament and set up an appointment for me with a loan officer at his bank in Massachusetts. At this particular time, no one could have had any more determination than I. After explaining my situation and financial status, the loan officer told me to check back with him the following day. If in fact, what I told him was true, I could pick up my money. The following day, at the other end of my phone call, came the good news. "Come and get your money." It was all coming together. I was able to purchase the airplane, and soon, I would have my pilot's license.

A new problem arose. What instructor had enough flying time in such a hot, high performance airplane

THE BEGINNING OF A BUSH PILOT

as the Cessna 206, to qualify for teaching me in my own airplane. It was a case of where I was the one to check the instructor out in how to fly my airplane so he could spend time supposedly instructing me. What a farce, but necessary, as I needed more dual time before getting my license.

I became more proficient with the Cessna 206, doing all my cross country flights required, including some instrument flying, building the hours almost on an every day basis.

With my written exam out of the way, it was only a short time later that I passed my check ride and received my pilots license. I immediately went to studying for my commercial license, and without the benefit of going to ground school, successfully passed my written and flight test.

Pilots at the airport were telling me to slow down. They seemed to think I was rushing my new found love for flying a little too fast. They began spreading rumors that I was not taking the time to learn, that I was a dangerous pilot, and whatever else they could think of. I just let them think they knew what they were talking about. After all, who but me, really knew what my capabilities were.

I knew what I wanted to do and I was going to do it. Even people in my home town had the story going around that I must be flying drugs, otherwise, how could I afford the airplane. It did seem like every dollar I earned or borrowed went into my flying.

I thought to myself many times, I must sacrifice in order to do what I have dreamed of doing for so many years. My dad used to tell me how he wanted to do

THE BEGINNING OF A BUSH PILOT

the very same thing I am working so hard for. He mentioned how he, as a young man and his friends designed and built a glider. How he was elected to fly it off a high hill first. Somehow, he lost control of the glider as he came down the hill, looped and crashed upside down, braking several bones. That was the extent of his adventure in flying, for in later years, as his dream too, could have been filled, his life unfortunately ended at an early age. It is with his dreams, and our closeness that I continue my pursuit of becoming a bush pilot.

Winter came, and the lake near where I lived had frozen over. I kept a plowed runway on the lake during the winter months giving me my own private air strip. I thought it would be nice to have the airplane closer to home and possibly gain more experience. Perhaps I could even add a few thrills along with it.

One time after a big snow fall, the strip I used for a runway had gotten shorter and very narrow. My brother Wayne, stood there shaking his head, saying. "You will never get your airplane out of there, that is way too short." The strip was just wide enough for the wheels of the airplane to fit between the snowbanks.

Challenges, I like. With the cool winter air and a long warm up, I lowered the flaps to twenty degrees and shoved the throttle all the way to full position. As I watched the wings skipping over the snow banks, it seemed the airplane hardly got going down the icy runway when it popped into the air like it had a jet booster attached to it, to fly free as a bird.

Nothing seemed too difficult for me. My adrenalin was running on high, so whatever encounters there

THE BEGINNING OF A BUSH PILOT

were, I met with little sweat. Flying, was definitely a natural to me. It was my high. Though I tell everyone I am scared of heights, it is such a wonderful feeling to slip down the face of a mountain, or float free as a bird around the countryside watching the beautiful bright orange sunset disappearing beyond the horizon. Best of all, there are no radar traps, stop signs, or traffic lights to worry about.

Flying had become a form of freedom, letting me forget my daily problems. To fly as the birds do, looking out over the vast country seeing sights one never sees from the ground.

March of the following year brought me back to the bank that financed my airplane. Speaking to the loan officer, I explained why my airplane needed a set of floats to earn its keep. Otherwise, it wasn't any good to me, that I needed money to purchase them with. My main objective, was to be a bush pilot and fly sportsmen into northern Canada hunting and fishing. I laid it on the line to him, and to my pleasure, I walked out with a sizable check in full for a new set of PK Floats.

Being early spring, some fast work had to be done. While the floats were being shipped, I had the task of converting what was originally a landplane, to a seaplane. No person to my knowledge, or anyone else's had ever converted a Cessna 206. Determination, and my mechanical background turned out to be a great asset. It seemed strange, that from all the airports and seaplane bases I had contacted, they all said I couldn't convert my 206 over to a seaplane. I had even called the FAA to inquire if they had a regu-

THE BEGINNING OF A BUSH PILOT

lation concerning my problem. But they had nothing in writing, so I convinced them, it must be okay.

A trailer truck pulls into the yard of my garage with two long crates aboard. My floats had arrived with all the fittings, spreader bars, bolts, and plans to assemble them. All other work at the garage was put on hold while the floats were assembled. Though hectic, it was a long and tedious job between taking care of customers at the gas pumps and all.

I was also working long hours trying to finish converting the airplane to floats before spring slipped away. Then one day, some guy stopped in at the garage and offered me five hundred dollars for my floats that were parked on my lawn. He either thought I was a dummy, or he was thinking they were floats for a dock. Five hundred dollars wouldn't buy the spreader bars for the floats. "Oh well."

Spring flew by, and the need for me to get a float rating became urgent. I have always been quite a dreamer, and for once, dreaming came in handy getting prepared for my float rating. Night after night, I would dream of flying a seaplane. Doing landings, takeoffs, and all the things pertinent to performing the operation of a seaplane. I must have done thousands of these things in my dreams before arriving at Folsom's seaplane base at Greenville, Maine where I was to get checked out by a seaplane instructor.

"Charlie," was a short, medium built guy, a person who had been around seaplanes for years. He was known as an instructor with a little too much high pressure and being very tough on his clients. Needless to say, he was assigned to give me some float

THE BEGINNING OF A BUSH PILOT

instructions. I had chosen Folsom's seaplane base because they had a Cessna 206 like mine. I thought it would be to my advantage.

Charlie jumped into the copilot's seat, and I, into the pilot's seat. While taxiing away from the dock, we swapped a few comments before I was told that familiar phrase, "show me what you know." That long, awaited moment had come. This is what I had been learning how to fly for. Thoughts about all my dreams of flying a seaplane were racing through my mind. Now is the time to put them to use. I kept my cool, and after a brief warm up of the engine, I pushed forward on the throttle and brought the control back in my lap.

As the seaplane plowed through the water with a nose high attitude, water sprayed out from under the floats. I had to keep the seaplane straight with the use of the rudder due to the torque and rotation of the engine. As the speed increased, I relaxed the pressure on the controls somewhat, allowing the seaplane to level out. Glancing my eyes at the air speed and other instrument gauges to see if all was well, when the seaplane reached about sixty miles per hour, I popped it off the water with the realization it was my first takeoff on floats.

Charlie was quick to give different instructions. He would tell me to do spot landings at particular points of land along the shores of the upper end of Moosehead Lake. Other times, he would reach over and pull the throttle back and tell me to make a dead stick landing. The worst part of the instructions, was when he told me to do fast step turns that could cause a person to wonder if the seaplane would flip over. A step turn, is when you make a turn under fast power, skimming along on top of the water almost at takeoff speed. This method is used primarily in short ponds where a pilot doesn't have a long enough straight run for takeoff. I personally have found it not to be very helpful in my situations. This was all in the routine of learning how to fly a seaplane.

After twelve or thirteen takeoffs and landings, and a good two hours of listening to Charlie, we finally returned to the seabase. I felt good about my performance. Charlie could not believe I did so well for not having flown on floats before. He asked me about that as we stepped out of the seaplane. He said he had never met a person that did so well in all his career of instructing. I told him, "it must have been because of all my dreaming." He laughed about that one, and wished me good luck. One more accomplishment, and one more step closer to fulfilling my dreams of becoming a bush pilot.

My next priority, was to install the floats on my airplane. There was a bit of hassle getting an overwidth load permit to transport the floats to Post Mills airport in Vermont from my garage in New Hampshire. The floats measured eleven and one half feet in width taking up a good share of the road. A special permit had to be obtained, but I managed that.

Before installing the floats, I spent several days putting the last finishing touches to the airplane. Cables had to be strung, and the necessary fittings and pulleys put in their proper places. Once again, anoth-

THE BEGINNING OF A BUSH PILOT

er big day had come. My maginificent 206 was parked on a dolly, ready to go.

Lake Fairlee was a mile down the road. We had to tow the airplane several hundred feet through a field and down a black top road, dodging trees, wires and telephone poles to a boat launching ramp where we slid the airplane into the water.

Now, I could put to use the experience I had acquired. Both at Greenville Maine and in my dreams. Though the instructor at Post Mills airport had not flown a 206 before, nor had he a seaplane rating, he agreed to ride shotgun with me. Years ago, a person could get away with a lot of things without consulting the rules. There wasn't many questions asked, but today, it is a different story.

I chose the Connecticut River to do my testing of the airplane with its newly equipped floats. I did several landings and takeoffs with no problems, while at the same time enjoying the new feeling of my Cessna 206 on floats. It seemed to fly more solidly and found I could set it on the river just about anywhere I pleased.

Dropping back onto Lake Fairlee, I thanked the instructor for his time and was on the phone immediately arranging to meet an FAA designate at the Merrimack River in Hooksett, NH within the hour. Mr. Ferns, owner and operator of a flying business at the Concord airport was the FAA designate and flew to a small discontinued airstrip next to the Merrimack River to give me my check ride. I didn't waste any time getting there. Mr. Ferns was just stepping out of his airplane as I pulled up to the shore.

THE BEGINNING OF A BUSH PILOT

The next forty five minutes consisted of several takeoffs and landings, stalls and turns. I was being scrutinized closely by a man that took flying seriously, and am sure he would not endorse my license unless he was satisfied with my performance. When it was all over and with a smile on his face, Mr. Ferns asked me for my pilot's license. I was soon on my way back home with my license signed and the ratings of Single Engine, Land and Sea. Happy to have achieved part of my dreams, and now, finally, on to my new adventures.

My adrenalin was flowing this day. Being only mid day, I hurriedly explained to my wife I was leaving for Canada. Would she mind watching the business for a few days. The urge to fly north was so intense, nothing could have stood in my way. If necessary, I think I would have closed the garage in order to go.

Neglecting my business was not the right thing to do. But, I had urgent business on my mind, and time was wasting. It would be a two and one half hour flight to my first destination.

The gathering of my fishing gear, tent, sleeping bag and survival gear was done in record time. I kissed my wife good-bye and headed for the dock where my 206 Cessna was waiting, almost as anxious as I was. All this had taken place over a matter of a few hours, having done the last finishing touches installing the floats and getting my seaplane rating. Determination had won out. It was like an unimaginable force had prevailed over me in order to get things done.

THE BEGINNING OF A BUSH PILOT

Green behind the ears and full of vim and vigor, I arrived at a seabase at St. Michael Des Saints, a hundred miles north of Montreal, Quebec. St. Michael Des Saints is a small settlement at the end of the road. A jumping off place for sportsmen to head off into the wilderness for hunting or fishing. It is dependent on tourists and logging, as well as sportsmen and outfitter camps scattered throughout the area with several Provincial parks. The seaplane base provides the air transportation by use of float planes into the north country.

After pulling up to the dock, I was greeted by several bush pilots wanting to get a glimpse of one of the first 206 Cessnas around. Questions were being asked left and right, but I was having difficulty understanding their French. They were happy to be allowed to look into the cockpit to gaze at the instrument panel with all the IFR equipment. Little did I realize how seldom some of the instruments would be used with the kind of flying I was about to do.

Pride was beaming inside me, but my easy going, nonchalant way kept me from showing it. To those that spoke English, I answered their questions to the best of my ability without letting on as to my inexperience. I was standing amongst an elite group of bush pilots, hoping some day, I too, would earn the right to be in such a prestigious group.

Survival, was the key word for this group of pilots that would dare fly in the roughest of weather conditions. Wind, rain, fog and snow, and lord knows what else. Respect for Mother Nature, was the almighty important factor to survival. That you may live to see

THE BEGINNING OF A BUSH PILOT

the sun set once again. That is, if the day was not overcast.

Flying in the North Country was to bring many challenges. There would be moments a pilot would have to call upon every bit of experience and coolness he could muster. Conditions that would put the very best of bush pilots to their greatest test. Some, would never make it beyond their first year. Others, that became too bold, or used poor judgment, may not make it through the day. Those that used their head, or had a little luck on their side, were called survivors. There is a saying around the North Country. "There are old bush pilots, and there are young bush pilots, but there are no, old, bold bush pilots."

The day was drawing to a close. A phone call to a Game Warden friend who lived in the nearby town of St. Michael Des Saints brought him to the seaplane base in a hurry. The next thing I knew, we were flying around the mountains and lakes looking at moose feeding in beaver ponds, or standing in bogs chomping on swamp grass or lily pads. I had no map of the area and soon found my first challenge of the North Country.

Darkness was soon approaching. We were having so much fun, I had forgotten to keep my bearings. Especially, as to where we were in relation to the seaplane base. There was little help from my Game Warden friend, he was lost in his own back yard. He was telling me how different everything looked from above. There was reason for concern because darkness was setting in, and we were getting low on fuel. My years of hunting, studying the sky and having to

THE BEGINNING OF A BUSH PILOT

memorize hills, finally paid off. We eventually made it back to the seabase, intact, and not much gas to spare, as darkness closed in.

Ben, my Game Warden friend, invited me to stay the night at his house, but not before putting together a plan to gather up two of his friends to fly to Hudson Bay the following day. So-called official business at a private fishing club a few miles out of town found us inside a beautiful log cabin lodge sitting beside a lake full of tasty brook trout. After a brief introduction to a tall, slender man in his fifties toting a small mustache, we found ourselves deeply indulged in discussing a fishing trip to Hudson Bay. So far..., so good.

Fred, the manager of the fishing club, the man I had just been introduced to, spoke of another person by the name of Phil who worked for Consolidated Paper Co.. He just happened to be staying at a motel in town. Things were really clicking. It just goes to show you, I don't think I had much to say about all this planning. Someone, was doing it for me. Like it had all been planned long before. A short visit with Phil, and some grocery shopping ended the evening with plans set to leave for Hudson Bay the following morning.

Across the lake from the seabase, the sun was slowly rising over the hill. The last few patches of fog were fast disappearing from above the cool waters. I was giving the seaplane its final inspection. Fuel tanks were topped off, floats checked for any water, and all our gear was packed aboard in its proper place. We bided our time while rechecking the newly acquired flight maps necessary for the trip.

THE BEGINNING OF A BUSH PILOT

Seeing the floats riding so low in the water, reminded me I had not been fortunate enough to afford a longer seaplane propeller. Subsequently, a much greater takeoff distance would be required, perhaps bringing us a few extra hectic moments and sweat. Big load, or not, we weren't going to let a little matter like that stand in our way.

Though hot days and big loads are a bush pilots nightmare, I shrugged off the possibilities of the short land plane propeller giving us any trouble I couldn't handle. It is up to the pilot to load his airplane accordingly. His judgment, his error. Many people who take a trip back into the North Country seem to think they have to bring all their belongings, including the kitchen sink. Always afraid they won't have enough of this, or that.

We were anxiously wanting to get started on our big adventure, so said our good-byes to the crew at the seabase. I taxied to the farthest corner of the lake, knowing full well we would need every inch of it for takeoff. Only after a thorough runup and a check of the instruments, did I go to full throttle to find us lumbering down the lake with one eye on the airspeed indicator and the other on the end of the lake which was coming up fast. This was my first experience flying a big load on floats and it had to be with a short propeller.

There was no turning back on this one. At the very end of the lake, with only a few feet to spare, just as we were lifting off, we gathered up a few lily pads with the floats, narrowly missing the roof tops at the edge of town. With the lily pads dangling from the floats,

THE BEGINNING OF A BUSH PILOT

we headed north west towards our destination, six hours flying time, north.

With nothing but wilderness, lakes, and mountains ahead, we flew for three hours to arrive at a seabase located on the river at Matagami. Beyond the sea-base, high towering power lines spanned the river over a large dam. The town was supported by a mining company. Indians had gathered on the dock, curiously looking on as I quickly secured the seaplane with ropes. Ben, Phil, and Fred stepped out of the seaplane, eyeing the Indians with suspicion. We had too many valuable cameras and other items on board to lose this early in the trip. We had previously been warned to keep our eyes and ears open at all times when the Indians are around.

Huge single engine Otters, along with several Dehaviland Beavers were parked at the dock. These seaplanes are the work horses of the North Country, dating back to the forties and fifties. Large radial engines supplied the power to carry their big loads.

Two or three men approached my seaplane with great interest, asking all sorts of questions about my 206, wanting to look inside. They seemed thrilled to notice all the instruments while remarking they had never seen a 206 on floats. I was trying to be modest about it all, but when one of them asked me how much float time I had, that was the kicker. These guys were big time bush pilots with thousands of hours. When they heard me mention I only had about seven hours on floats, they could not believe it. I had to say something in my defense. I told them I was a firm believer in experience being the best teacher. Their

THE BEGINNING OF A BUSH PILOT

remark to that, was. "Don't worry, you will get plenty of that, flying up in the North Country."

There I was, absolutely green behind the ears, but with all the dreams and ambition of being a great bush pilot. Little did I know how much their statement would reflect on me, time, and time again.

I had used up one full tank of fuel flying from St. Michael Des Saints to Matagami. It would take all of the fuel from the other tank to get us to Fort George, at Hudson Bay. I had no intention of flying a known distance without extra fuel in case of bad weather or some other unforeseen problem, so began looking into the possibility of refueling the empty tank.

The dispatcher, who was in a small shack used for an office, told me how lucky I was. He had only one drum of 100/130 octane aviation gas left, which was out around the corner of the building. "That was fine with me, " I said. "What I don't use now, I will get on the way back." No one seemed too anxious to help show me the drum of fuel. Being the first time ever to fuel the seaplane from a drum, I was not aware of a lot of the problems one could run into. It seems, people at these northern seaplane bases are careless when it comes to keeping fuel in fifty five gallon drums. You may find water, rust, fuel oil, jet fuel, or if you are lucky, it could be aviation gas. The next thing, is to check the color as to what octane rating it is. If it was green, it is 100/130 octane. A reddish color would indicate it is automobile gas, or 80/87 octane. The newer low lead gas is blue. If the gas was oily when you rub your fingers in it, that would more likely be outboard motor gas premixed with oil.

THE BEGINNING OF A BUSH PILOT

Well, we found the one drum marked aviation gas, 100/130 and rolled it down to the dock. Using a portable pump and a funnel with a filter, we managed to get the seaplane refueled. Thanking the operator that sold us what I thought to be good old aviation gas, we climbed back into the seaplane to be on our way.

The temperature had climbed into the nineties and that spelled trouble. Knowing we had to taxi a long way down the river, we took the opportunity to eat our lunch. We taxied around bend after bend, until I figured we had gone three miles or so. That should give us enough room to take off, I hoped. The picture of the power lines over the river kept flashing in my mind. Hitting those would be the last thing we wanted to do.

Takeoff, was long and difficult. There was no wind. The temperature was in the nineties, and the water was glassy. That, coupled with the problem of a short propeller not pulling enough air, wasn't helping our situation. Finally, with an extra prayer and patting the dash, telling my newly named (SweetLips) seaplane, "lets go," we slowly lifted off, barely having enough altitude to clear the power lines. Wiping the sweat off our foreheads, we all sat back to relax and look forward to what was to come next.

Hills, flat swampy areas, rivers and lakes, pass us by. Short and stunted black spruce trees were seen in abundance with an occasional cluster of birch or poplar trees. Moose were seen in the sanctuary of beaver ponds seeking to avoid the pesky flies and to cool their bodies. Beaver ponds also provided a lot of vegetation contained in the diet of the moose where

THE BEGINNING OF A BUSH PILOT

downed poplar trees crisscrossing the edge of the water provided small branches and buds for food. Raspberry bushes growing in these areas also provided plenty of nourishment for the moose.

As our flight progressed, the terrain gave way to flatter country. Other than a few small hills jutting up two to four hundred feet high, there was nothing but marsh land and few trees. Here and there, we were able to see a small pond. The Rupert River flowed into James Bay past an Indian village named Prince Rupert. Only a few hundred Indians existed there with the aid of the Hudson Bay Trading Company and a few white personnel to operate the two way radio equipment.

James Bay is known world wide for its goose hunting. The geese spend their summers there, raising their young, and leaving in September to fly south for the winter. Almost every body of water, whether small or large, had a family of geese in it. We took special notice of the male geese standing guard with their necks stretched high on the lookout for some animal after its meal. Wolves, Fox, Mink, and sometimes northern pike, eat their share of baby geese, but I suppose that is all figured in the balance of Mother Nature.

Navigation had become a bit of a problem. At this time, due to lack of navigational aids in this part of the country, I was literally flying by the seat of my pants. My flight map indicated lakes, rivers and mountains, but when there were none of those to be seen, there was only miles and miles of flat, swampy territory. There wasn't much for land marks to focus

THE BEGINNING OF A BUSH PILOT

on for navigating. I soon discovered, if I flew low, over the ground, I could use the small, two to four hundred foot hills that jutted up, as reference points. Between them and my compass, I could manage to navigate.

We eventually could look off to our west and see the shoreline of James Bay as we passed over other Indian villages. This was wild country. No other civilization or roads scarred this vast, untamed country of the North.

Summers were short, and the winters long. All food supplies had to be flown in, or brought by ship that came once a year after ice out. The soil could not support growing vegetables, nor could the short season and cold weather permit it.

A small Indian settlement appeared ahead of us. It lay at the top of a hill overlooking Hudson Bay next to one lonely dirt air strip. We were to land at a seabase located on the LaGrande River that circled the south end of the Indian village and emptied into Hudson Bay. Several seaplanes were parked at a large dock belonging to the seabase where we were to land. The village looked deserted at first, but as we circled over the roof tops, the sound of our engine brought people out of their shacks wondering who the strangers were. Indians had gathered at the dock waiting for our arrival. They wanted to see who dared venture this far north.

Fort George, a desolate, windswept Indian outpost, lay on the southeastern shore of Hudson Bay. This, was to be our place of communication with the outside world. We had successfully made it to our destination. Looks of curiosity and smiles greeted us

THE BEGINNING OF A BUSH PILOT

at the dock after our professional looking landing on the river, laden with strong, swirling currents. The few pilots employed by Fecteau Air Ltd. strolled down from the office to shake hands and inquire as to our needs. I explained, we needed a place to stay for the night, as they helped secure the seaplane.

Once again, the Cessna 206 became the center of attraction. One thing for sure, I had chosen the proper aircraft for my adventures of a bush pilot. This seaplane was to prove itself for its comfort, speed, and performance for years to come.

Once all the Indians disappeared back into their shacks, we all enjoyed the celebration of our arrival, swapping stories with our newly found Canadian pilot friends, along with their warm welcome. They didn't get many visitors and seemed quite intent on catching up on any news from civilization that we could give them.

Discussions of where to fish the next day, where to eat and sleep kept us busy that evening. There was difficulty in keeping track of time. Being the first part of July and that far north, it didn't get very dark at night. We were told we could sleep for one dollar a night at the school and get something to eat there.

The pilots had invited us back for a party they were having later, mentioning there would be some pretty Indian girls there as well. Thanking them for all their help, we locked the doors of the seaplane, hoping our equipment would be safe.

While walking along the trail through the Indian village, we noticed several old snowmobiles, mostly Skidoos sitting beside shabby looking prefab build-

THE BEGINNING OF A BUSH PILOT

ings. A few teepees that had been erected here and there, were used mostly for storage. A few fires were seen outside the Indian homes used for cooking up some caribou meat or fish. The Cree Indians seemed very shy. As we met them on the trail, they would turn their head to avoid eye contact.

Locating the school, we searched out the person in charge to square away the problem of sleeping and food for the night. We managed to arrange for two rooms to rest our weary bodies, but getting something to fill our starving stomachs was to be another problem. We were told there was supposed to be a restaurant close by. We thought a steak or two, and home fries might be real tasty.

Searching the area, we came upon a small ranch type building where the air was filled with the scent of food being cooked. Opening the door, brought us into a single room with a counter next to a grill. Our expectations of a steak supper had dwindled to a hamburger and coke, hardly enough to satisfy four hungry men. We would have to depend on fresh caught trout the following day. I guess the cost of shipping in steaks from such a great distance prohibited having steaks on the menu.

The Indian Chief was the big boss of that small village of Crees at Fort George. We needed a two way portable HF radio to take with us for a few days and was told he was the one to see. While the pilots at the seabase were busy with their party, expecting us to show up, we were busy chatting with the old Indian Chief. Ben was using his authority to get the loan of a radio and some information on where to go

THE BEGINNING OF A BUSH PILOT

fishing. Visiting with the Chief until the early hours of the morning caused us to miss the party. Personally, I really didn't care about getting involved in a drinking party involving some Indian girls. Fishing was more important than getting into trouble over an Indian gal. Besides, I was married and didn't drink.

Five o'clock in the morning seemed a bit early, but looking forward to catching six to eight pound speckled brook trout had us fully awake and anxious to fly eighty miles north of Fort George. Seal River was suppose to have some of the finest speckled trout fishing in the world.

At the seabase, I roused the pilots out of their short sleep from a late party. I couldn't help notice several Indian girls as they slid under their covers, disappearing from sight. While helping us get organized, one of the pilots remarked about how nice the party was. Before leaving, I obtained a flight map showing the area we intended to fish, assuring us we could find our way back to Fort George, providing problems didn't arise.

Having inspected the floats and the aircraft to see if all was in readiness for departure, I attempted to start the engine. Much to everyone's dismay, it refused to start. Raw fuel dripped from the exhaust pipes, indicating it was getting plenty of fuel. Spark was getting to the spark plugs. That was a new one on me. The engine had always started instantly and I could see no reason for it not to, then. This far north, the nights are very cold the first of July, but that was little cause for this problem. Our plan for an early departure was not to be, as the continuous cranking of the

THE BEGINNING OF A BUSH PILOT

starter drained the last bit of life from the battery.

Ben suggested, perhaps the Indian Chief could supply us with a booster battery from a bulldozer they had in the village. Sure enough, the Chief obliged us. An hour later, with the help of the large booster battery, the Cessna 206 engine roared to life, bringing sweet music to our ears. Broad smiles replaced the long faces we had shared earlier. Not totally satisfied, it was decided I should test the seaplane before we left for "no-man's land."

Phil, Fred and Ben stayed behind while I flew around the area to checkout the seaplane. I noticed a higher than normal fuel flow being indicated on the gauge as well as a cooler engine temperature. Other than that, there seemed to be good power as I flew over the seabase, tipping the wings to the gang at the dock. Seeing my friends waiving, and the anxiety to go fishing, took away any further concerns I had. After landing the seaplane, I restarted the engine several times to be sure everything was okay.

We thanked the pilots for their help and told them we would bring them back some fish and proceeded to take off towards our destination to Seal River. As we flew north, I carefully studied the flight map laid across my lap showing the many lakes and rivers. I was busy comparing what was on the map to what we were seeing below. The visibility was fantastically clear. Hundreds of tiny Islands dotted the shoreline along Hudson Bay. As we looked inland, we could see thousands of lakes glittering in the early morning sun. River after river could be seen winding their way westward through the terrain to their final destination

THE BEGINNING OF A BUSH PILOT

into Hudson Bay.

We had already ventured further north than most people. And there are those that know very little of the existence of this territory, and its resources.

The four of us joked and chatted as we ate our breakfast of sandwiches and fruit while gathering in the amazing sight of the desolate, wild and unforgiving North Country. The Cessna 206 purred like a kitten, taking us over poorly charted territory, leaving Fort George, our last human contact, further behind. Whenever a likely fishing spot would appear, such as rapids containing deep holes, we would swoop down to check them out.

At one point, we came upon a wrecked seaplane. We pondered over the fate of its crew while investigating the wreckage and to wonder why it crashed, or who it s occupants may have been, or if in fact they survived. Numerous accidents occur for many reasons throughout northern Canada. As long as man seeks adventure, he will continue to put himself at risk against the many elements that may confront him. The river close to the crash site was cold and too rampant from the melting snow and ice to do any fishing, so we flew on in search of more appealing places.

An abandoned camp on the Rogan River was our next stop. A sandy beech close by provided a safe haven for the seaplane. It was free from rocks that could easily cause damage to the floats and would be safe in case of strong winds. Plus, it was handy for unloading our supplies.

THE BEGINNING OF A BUSH PILOT

Nearby, a raging torrent of water tumbled down over huge waterfalls to form a mass of white foam. The powerful force of the water bouncing off the rocks shot spray high in the air, providing us with a spectacular sight.

After tightly securing the seaplane, Ben and Fred grabbed their fly rods, Phil and I, our spinning rods and we all headed out to go fishing. It was only a matter of minutes before the sound of rushing water was dominated by yells and cheers. Everyone was catching fish almost every cast. Beautiful speckled brook trout leaped far out of the water, shaking their heads frantically, trying to free themselves from the hook at the end of our lines. Brook trout, ranging from three to six pounds and greater were plentiful, and could be seen swimming back and forth in the crystal clear water.

We attempted to fish the great waterfall, but the water was so furious, we could hardly notice a fish on the line. White spray danced in the air as water tumbled over the falls, splashing and bouncing off the rocks below. One slip of our feet and we could soon become a victim of the icy waters. It is best to fish with a buddy when fishing the big rivers if one wants to survive.

The remainder of the day was spent fishing the Rogan River. Daylight was of no concern, as it was present almost twenty four hours a day, so we continued fishing until our stomachs started calling for food. On the ledge next to the river's edge, we built an open fire to enjoy a feast of delicious tasty trout cooked to a golden brown in a butter laden skillet.

THE BEGINNING OF A BUSH PILOT

While eating our fill, we discussed events of the trip to date. We related to the fantastic fishing, of which none of us had ever experienced.

The Seal River was also on my mind for the following day. How would the fishing there compare to what we had on the Rogan River. A fire was built in an old beat up stove at the abandoned camp to keep the frost out and to warm our noses a little before crawling into the sleeping bags for the night.

The following morning brought the same kind of problems we experienced at Fort George. Once again, the engine of the 206 would not start. There we were, a hundred miles from help. The airplane's battery was dead, and lord only knows what else could be wrong. There must have been some sort of jinx over us, trying to keep us from getting to Seal River.

For whatever the reason, I was having a difficult time analyzing the problem of the seaplane. My attempts to start the engine had failed. Could we have gotten a bad batch of gas at Matagami? I remember the dispatcher saying how lucky we were, it was the last drum of aviation gas he had of 100/130. Fortunately, we had borrowed an HF Radio from our good friend the Indian chief at Fort George just in case of such an emergency.

After exhausting all other efforts to find the probble, I drained a portion of fuel from the fuel tank to inspect it. A strange odor came to my nose, detecting something other than gas. The smell of alcohol was quite apparent. To verify my suspicion, I mixed it with water and watched it turn milky color. There was little doubt I had found the problem that had given us so

THE BEGINNING OF A BUSH PILOT

much trouble.

Realizing that Matagami was the last place I had taken on fuel, things began to come clear. I purposely did not refuel at Fort George in order to keep the weight down on account of the short land plane prop. Less load would allow us to fly in and out of more fishing areas, plus the fact we didn't have all that far to fly. Someone, had evidently used a drum marked aviation gas to store alcohol in. It is a deicing fluid, mainly used for deicing airplanes during the winter, as well as adding to fuel to help prevent moisture. This surely was a lesson for me to remember as long as I live.

Ben, repeatedly tried to call Fort George on the HF radio, but got no response. Finally, the voice of the radio operator at Fort Rupert came over the radio to say. "I will try to reach Fort George and pass on your distress message." We needed at least ten gallons of gas and a booster battery to get us out of our situation.

While waiting for help to arrive, I decided to switch to the opposite tank. I could control which tank I drew fuel from by a selector valve located between the two front seats. With the little amount of good gas I had left, I flooded the system and cranked the engine. It started immediately. There was my proof.

Several hours had passed before we heard the welcoming sound of an airplane approaching from the south. Help was on the way. Within a short time, we were happily greeting one of the pilots from Fort George by the name of Richard Trombley. He spoke of the difficulty they often had with radio communica-

THE BEGINNING OF A BUSH PILOT

tions due to weather conditions.

It didn't take long for the news to travel throughout northern Quebec about an American being sold alcohol for his seaplane by mistake. The pilot strongly suggested it would be best for us to follow him back to Fort George to get things squared away. We could refuel with good gas and come back later. That sounded okay to us. Seal River would have to wait once again. So.., after packing up, Fred jumped into the seaplane belonging to Fecteau Co., to keep the pilot company and off we went, flying side by side back to Fort George.

Fecteau Aviation was afraid of a law suit stemming from their mistake on the alcohol situation. The manager at the seabase at Fort George was given instructions to be sure to give me whatever I needed free of charge. No one knew for sure if the alcohol would damage my engine, but they didn't want to upset me, either. I would be given free gas and oil for the taking in hopes of no further repercussions.

Several Indians had gathered around the dock looking for some kind of handout, so I gave them some of our fish. The next thing I knew, they were up by their camp whipping up a fire to cook their fish. Others hung around just to see what was going on.

I had no place to drain the alcohol from the wing tank of the seaplane, but into the river. When this started happening, the Indians scrambled for a boat and buckets to catch the alcohol. They had to pay six dollars a gallon when they buy it at the Hudson Bay Trading Company. When they decide to get together for a party, they mix the alcohol with water to make what they call "fire water" to drink. "Yuk. What else?" It was illegal for them to have liquor in the Indian villages, but no one made any attempt to stop them. All I could think of, was the village water pipe that led into the river beside the seaplane where the alcohal was draining. We were all chuckling about that one, thinking the people in the village would would be feeling pretty good, come night. After the last drops were caught, the Indians disappeared in a hurry. I set out to refuel and double check the seaplane. We would spend the night at the school and hopefully fly to Seal River the following morning.

Evening time gave us a chance to relax and get to know more about the remote Indian village so far north. The school where we were staying, was the only source of education for the Indians up and down the coastline of Hudson and James Bay.

Throughout the warm summer months, the Indians spend their time camping and fishing with their families among the many Islands and travel by boat up the rivers to look for fish and game. When winter comes, in early September and October, the Indians gather up their children from all around to live and go to school at Fort George. The Parents of these children would go their separate ways out into what we call, "no-man's land" to do their hunting and trapping. Snowmobiles had replaced most of the sled dogs, as we had seen several parked by each Indian home.

While walking through the village, sounds of violins and other music led us to a fairly large building. To our surprise, we saw Indian men dancing to a good old fashion ho-down. We made our way inside

THE BEGINNING OF A BUSH PILOT

and stood quietly, noticing their dark, weatherbeaten faces studying us as the music continued. Two nights a week, the village people gathered for their entertainment.

Once a year the Indians look forward to fresh supplies, if and when a lone ship is able to make it's way through the ice in the Hudson Strait. Food supplies were expensive, along with everything else. In the Spring and Fall the Indians would sell the geese they hunted to the Hudson Bay Trading Co. for a price of twenty five cents each, only to turn around and pay two dollars or more that winter to buy one back. I thought someone was making a good profit on that one. That's Government for you.

It was interesting to see how different the Indian customs were, compared to ours, but the one thing that is the same world wide, we all get hungry. That took us back to the one and only restaurant. Perhaps this time, we could get a nice tasty steak with a few trimmings. I guess they must have forgotten to add steak to their menu. We were asked how many hamburgers we wanted, that we could have some french fries and a coke. No steak, no salad, or anything else. "Oh", we could have ice cream at a dollar per small scoop. We made up our mind, if we were to have a good meal, it would have to be cooked by us at Seal River the next day.

Getting an early start the following morning, posed little problem. We were prepared to go fishing, and the now famous Cessna 206 started promptly. As we flew north, scattered patches of fog shrouded the low land. Luckily for us, the weather was cooperatiing

THE BEGINNING OF A BUSH PILOT

nicely. A decision was made to take no detours. We would fly directly to Seal River. I closely referred to the flight map as we basically flew the same route as the previous day. Recognizing many of the lakes we had seen earlier, we soon came upon the old campsite at Rogan River. Happy thoughts of the good fishing we had the day before were left behind as we approached a large river a short time later.

Seal River lay before us, stretching for miles from east to west. We had finally made it. We flew up and down the river, checking each rapid or waterfall for potential areas of good fishing. The seaplane was in its glory, and so were we. There were many natural landing strips available. Sections of the river were deep enough to land on, as well as the lakes that the river flowed in and out of. I just had to keep an eye out for that hidden rock.

It was one of these such lakes that I chose to land on. The river was wide, and shallow enough for us to wade, making it ideal for fly fishing. I landed as close to the mouth of the river as I dared without getting caught up in the swift current. Otherwise, we might have found ourselves floating down the river and getting hung up on some rocks. That didn't sound like it was something I was interested in seeing happening. When so far from help, it was better to use caution.

The fishing couldn't wait any longer. We tied the seaplane in a safe spot and went on the run, carrying our fishing rods in one hand and some snacks in the other, to see who was going to land the first fish. At the mouth of the river, a smooth, but steady flow of

THE BEGINNING OF A BUSH PILOT

water found its way over and around rocks that were covered with a greenish moss. We were reminded constantly of the icy, cold water when we stepped on the slippery rocks causing us to lose our balance and fall head first or backwards into the water giving us the surprise of our life. Fires had to be built to dry our clothes. It seemed to take forever to dry our boots.

The clear water made it easy for us to see huge speckled trout darting among the rocks jutting out of the water. At times, the fish were all around me. I could feel them swimming against my boots. It was like we had found our own private fish hatchery.

Ben and Fred stood on some exposed rocks out in the middle of the river casting their chosen flies. It was a spectacular sight. Speckled trout seemed to hit about everything that hit the water. While Phil and I were busy playing the huge trout on the end of our lines, we could see trout leaping out of the water in front of Ben and Fred. There was no question about it, the fishing was the best we had ever seen. Better than at Rogan River, and we thought that was good.

With their huge square tails, five to eight pound trout were jumping out of the water catching flies among the bushes hanging out over the edge of the river. We could hear the splash "K..flop" as they fell back into the water.

Few sportsmen will experience the kind of fishing that we were having. No matter what part of the river we fished, trout after trout gave us a battle royal. Even as we waded from one section of the river to the other, we could feel the trout as they glanced off our boots. This had to be a fisherman's paradise. It was

THE BEGINNING OF A BUSH PILOT

quite a thrill to cast in close to shore under the over hanging bushes and have a big trout slam your hook and come flying out of the water shaking its head in a struggle to get free.

The Indians back at Fort George would all be lined up at the dock if they knew what kind of success we were having. We had intentions of bringing them back some extra fish, so I hoped they would be there to welcome us. The largest speckled brook trout I have caught in the area was eleven pounds, thirteen ounces. A Polish friend of mine from New Jersey with the name of Max, caught one that weighed eleven pounds. After spending half an hour fighting the fish and finally getting it in the net, he stood there smiling with admiration, then gently released it back into the river. I yelled at him, "why didn't you keep the fish, it will be the largest brook trout you will ever catch?" He remarked, "I don't care about keeping the big fish, I only like the small pan fries, their better for eating." I could not argue about that one. The problem was, we were not catching many small fish.

It had been a long and successful day of fishing. Though all of us had fallen in the river and gotten a good drenching, we had a great time. It was time to head back to Fort George. The thought of fog that usually plagues the coastline of Hudson Bay in the evening was nagging me so, I told my friends we had better get a move on. The fish had to be dressed and packed in the cold, moist moss to preserve them for the long trip home. We made sure the area was clean of any trash and loaded the gear into the seaplane, to say Bon Voyage to Seal River, and one fantastic experience.

Flying south towards Fort George, the closer we got to Hudson Bay and the seabase, the more fog we encountered. Either we were late leaving Seal River, or the fog had come in early.

Arriving at Fort George, we found ourselves in a touch and go situation. The only signs we could see of the village, was a few roof tops and chimneys protruding up through the dense fog. It can be a deadly game flying in such foggy conditions. A pilot prefers not to take too many chances if he cares about any longevity in his flying career.

As far as the eye could see, a massive blanket of white fog stretched out before us. The precious minutes of daylight that were passing by, only lessened our chances of finding a way onto the river to the seabase. After making several passes over the fog shrouded village, I was able to get a small glimpse of water as I peered into the fog. A quick decision, and barely clearing the rooftops, I found our way onto the river close to the seabase.

For a few minutes, it was like we were playing tag with some of the chimneys sticking up out of the fog from the Indian camps. The Indians must have gotten a thrill out of that. One thing for sure, I was getting a good education in bush flying, especially in the fog.

By now, the 206 Cessna was a welcome and familiar sight at Fort George. A sizable group of Indians had already gathered at the dock to greet us, hoping to receive a few fish. The extra fish we had on board brought big smiles as we passed them out. Carrying their supper in hand, the Indians quickly headed for

THE BEGINNING OF A BUSH PILOT

their homes.

This would be our last night at Fort George. We spent our free time visiting with the pilots at the seabase and later with the Indian Chief while returning the HF radio that had gotten us out of a jam earlier. Needless to say, so far, it had been quite an eventful trip. I had added a few more hours under my belt as a Bush Pilot and gained a lot of valuable experience that I would call on for years to come.

On our trip home, we explored other fishing areas to mark on my flight map for future use. We had to stop at Matagami for fuel, and was not surprised to hear the dispatcher at the seabase say. " Help yourself to the fuel, I prefer not to touch anything to do with fuel, in case something goes wrong. Just let me know when you are finished refueling the seaplane."

Afterwards, the dispatcher forced a smile or two, and was quick to tell me everything was free. I took the time to explain to him, "it was not my intention to sue Fecteau and Company." He made an apologetic speech, and bid us farewell, hoping it would be the last time he would see us. That of course, was just wishful thinking on his part, for little did he realize how soon he was to see me again in the weeks to follow.

Several hours later, after flying over nothing but wilderness, we were welcomed back by the crew at the seabase in St. Michael Des Saints. The smooth, relaxing flight from Matagami, climaxed a most successful and enjoyable fishing trip with my three Canadian friends. People gathered to see the huge trophy speckled brook trout displayed on the dock, while

THE BEGINNING OF A BUSH PILOT

the events of the last few days unfolded. Phil, Ben, and Fred spoke in French and English, depending on to whom they spoke, while I proudly stood by my Cessna 206, trying to understand their conversation. Whatever was being said in French was lighting up peoples faces, so it must have been good.

In a way, I hated to go back home to the dull life of my garage business and all its headaches. I was sure my wife had her fill of taking care of things in my absence. I end this story, only to say, that this was only the beginning of my bush pilot career. My many memories of the freedom and total enjoyment I spent flying around the North Country in a seaplane will always be present. To dream of the big ones that got away and to see the wonders of Mother Nature.

I also mention the kind hospitality of the Canadians that we encountered, including the help of the lonely radio operators in the remote areas of the North and the culture of the Cree Indians and other tribes. They are all part of the small amount of civilization that survive above the fifty second parallel, necessary to us that venture north.

BACK
TO SEAL RIVER

Since my first trip to Hudson Bay in northern Quebec, and having such a fantastic experience fishing at Seal River, it was difficult to keep my mind focused on my business. Going back to Seal River seemed to be all that I could think about. I needed to find someone interested in helping out on expenses, and maybe a little extra.

Luck came, when a customer friend of mine stopped at the garage one day who happened to be a pilot of twenty years, one of those I term as a weekend pilot. He was quite taken up with our discussion of fishing and learning of my Cessna 206 being on floats. The more we talked, the more excited and interested he became.

He was a big fellow, well over two hundred and fifty pounds. That gave me an excellent opportunity to bring up the subject of a longer and better performing seaplane propeller needed to replace the less efficient, shorter land plane propeller I was forced to fly with on my first trip up north.

67

BACK TO SEAL RIVER

My plea for a little financial help was successful. Arrangements were made, and in a matter of days, my wife and I, along with my pilot friend and his wife were lifting off Lake Sunapee, NH headed for Canada with a new shiny seaplane propeller installed. The difference between the two propellers was like night and day. The Cessna 206 lifted off the water so much quicker, it was like gaining a few more horse power. It was an understatement, to say I felt happy with the new performance. It relieved my mind somewhat, for having to carry heavy loads most of the time.

Weather posed little problem as we retraced the route I had flown earlier on my first trip, taking us past Montreal, on to St. Michael Des Saints, then to Matagami. The dispatcher at Matagami was so shocked to see me back, his jaw must have dropped six inches. He threw his hands in the air and told me, "help yourself to the fuel for the seaplane, I'll take the money when you get through gassing up." He wasn't about to touch any part of helping us. He was afraid we might get the wrong fuel again, such as the alcohol I was given by mistake on my first trip north.

We didn't waste much time getting out of Matagami. Though the day was hot with very little wind, we had no problem getting off the water as before. This time, we had plenty of leeway to clear the power lines that spanned the river near the seabase.

My passengers were enjoying their flight and feeling the freedom of the wide open spaces where little civilization existed. They got great pleasure in seeing all sorts of wild life, but found it hard to believe there could be so many lakes and rivers uninhabited by

BACK TO SEAL RIVER

man. We had seen an abundance of moose, and the further north we got, we began seeing caribou making there way across the tundra. We also had the opportunity of seeing families of geese swimming about close to their nesting place. There were times, when we happened to look above us, we would see a big bald eagle come diving past us to check us out. An occasional osprey was seen carrying a fish head first in its claws, and then land in a tree where a nest of little ones waited with open mouths.

We passed over, what seemed like an endless expanse of tundra, with the exception of a few scattered patches of black spruce trees stunted from the severe winters and short growing season. Spruce trees measuring only four to five inches in diameter, obtained the age of one hundred and thirty five years. The tree's (aging rings) are so close together, you need to use a magnifying lens and the sharp edge of a razor blade to count them. The North Country is a tough and unmerciful place that shows no favors to man or animal. It is only with respect that those who dare venture this far north can survive.

We flew across the great Rupert River where it emptied into the southeastern tip of James Bay near Rupert House. Then up along the coastline, passing over the East Main river where we looked down upon the few sparsely populated Indian villages. The familiar sight of thousands of lakes and streams brought back memories from only a few weeks past.

Fort George was not hidden under a blanket of fog this time. We arrived in full daylight, giving us a clear birdseye view of the Indian village and school,

BACK TO SEAL RIVER

where hopefully, we would be staying for a few days.

We were welcomed at the seabase by the Canadian pilots, quite surprised to see me back so soon. Some of the local Indians, whose interests seem to lie in watching for new arrivals, waited for a handout, or two. It was quite apparent to see the excitement and curiosity on the faces of my wife and friends. One could read the pleasure of their new adventure in their eyes as they looked around, marveling at the very existence of the remote Indian village along the shores of Hudson Bay.

First, we went to the school to get settled in our quarters. Later in the evening, I took them on a tour of the village to see the different Indian customs and the way they live in the North.

The following morning greeted us with plenty of sunshine. After checking our fishing gear and making sure our emergency supplies were intact, we headed for Seal River and a day of fishing.

As expected, our day was well rewarded with the thrill of catching some of the finest batch of trophy brook trout anywhere in Canada. It was easy fishing for the amateurs, as there seemed to be a fish waiting wherever a cast was made. Nowhere in southern Canada could we duplicate the fishing experience we enjoyed here on the Seal River. There was no end to the vast watershed that raised so many trophy fish.

Everyone was having so much fun, they paid no attention to what time of day it was. All the time, a white, grayish sky had been slowly creeping in on us. Fort George was close to an hour flying time away, so I hurried my wife and friends into the seaplane to

BACK TO SEAL RIVER

hopefully make it back before conditions deteriorated too much, forcing us to camp out in bad weather.

I chose to fly the coastline back, hoping to avoid the hills. If necessary, I could fly low over the water, staying under the fog. The further we went, the worse the conditions got. I was being forced to fly lower and lower, until I was barely missing the tiny rock islands jutting out of the water. My co-pilot, the pilot of twenty five years, had become so nervous and sweaty over the situation, he kept yelling at me to do this, or that. He sure wasn't keeping his cool. I finally had to put him in his place by telling him to shut his mouth and leave the flying to me. I had enough to contend with, without listening to him.

I felt quite sympathetic for everyone, under the circumstances, but it was plain to see, we were not going to make it much further following the coastline back to Fort George. The fog was down to the water's surface hiding the tiny islands that I earlier was able to fly around and between, giving me no choice but to turn back. With the wing tip pivoting within inches of the water, I made a tight turn north towards a hole in the fog where the sun poked through. It was tough flying, but all I can say is, we had a body of water under us to land on most of the time.

We managed to fly far enough inland to follow a river through all its twists and turns. At times, we were forced to fly at water level between the river banks because of low fog, before finally make it back to Fort George. As we pulled up to the dock, I took a look back in the direction of where we had just come, only to see the river completely obscured. Bush flying can get a little hairy at times, but it certainly calls for a cool head and a few "whews....."

We were surprised to see several private sea-planes at the seabase. A bad storm had stranded the sportsmen, but that wasn't their only problem. The pilots didn't know their way back to Montreal. They confronted me about the possibility of leading them back south to a certain point they could recognize when the weather cleared. I could see it was a case of a pilot helping another in trouble, so I kindly agreed to bail them out of their predicament. Maybe, if we got a break in the weather, we could get in some fishing on the way back home.

Two days had passed before the weather conditions finally improved. After a long discussion with the group of fishermen and their pilots, we decided to see if we could make it south. Small breaks in the overcast gave us some encouragement as we played follow the leader while keeping in radio contact and what visual contact was possible. I never cared much about trying to keep track of someone else following me, and an added three airplanes tripled my concerns. It became so hectic dodging low hanging fog, within a very few minutes we found ourselves all sitting on a beach wondering if we should have stayed at Fort George.

It was a beautiful spot for everyone to get acquainted and swap a few stories. As it turned out, we had one big picnic while waiting for the fog to lift.

Several hours passed during several attempts to leave the safety of the lake, as the fog did its thing, moving in and out. Once in a while, a hill top would

BACK TO SEAL RIVER

appear across the lake, giving us a little hope, only to disappear again. Finally, one of the pilots decided he would take his group up in his airplane and take a look around. His last statement was. "I will stay in radio contact with you."

An hour went by with no word from him or his friends. Fear set in among the remaining group, thinking for sure their friends had crashed. It was strange not to have heard any message from them. My first thought, was to get to the nearest Indian village and later search for the missing airplane. In one last attempt before the last hour of daylight left us, we managed to make it to a small Indian village called "Paint Hills." Much to our surprise, our missing friends were there, waiting.

The whole village turned out to welcome us. It was like a big celebration. We were surrounded by about sixty five Indians as their Chief escorted us to the main building. To help pass the evening, entertainment was supplied in the form of a good old fashion ho down, with a little music from fiddles and violins .

We had only managed to fly a total of fifty miles that day. The following morning, we poked our heads from our sleeping quarters and was greeted with a bright sun and clear skies. We were most appreciative for the hospitality of the Indians. Happy to have everyone together again, we got off with a cheery departure. This time, we would all stay together.

For the next few hundred miles, the radios were busy with French jokes, with a little English thrown in. We made our way south to a point of recognition by my followers in the three seaplanes, and as we part-

BACK TO SEAL RIVER

ed company, we wished them good luck. As for my group, we enjoyed more fishing on the way home, glad to take a break from all the bad weather.

For one reason or another, I am sure our wives will remember this trip for quite sometime. It must have been quite an experience for them, being their first time on an expedition of this sort so far north. There would be plenty of stories to be told upon their arrival at home.

CATCHING
THE BIG ONE

This is a story about catching one of those big speckled brook trout that always seems to get away, but not this one. On a return trip into the James Bay and Hudson Bay area during my first few years of flying north, I found myself, and those that dared fly with me having what you'd call "a real adventurous, one heck of a good time."

With our fishing gear, sleeping bags, tent, food, and the necessary survival items loaded into my 206 Cessna seaplane, myself and three friends had decided we would do some exploring in the North Country. There had to be a few huge trophy speckled brook trout lurking in the waters inland from James Bay and Hudson Bay area of northern Quebec.

The biggest concern of flying in such a remote territory, was the lack of fuel, or its availability. Though my seaplane had long range fuel tanks, plus the few spare cans of fuel we carried on board, running out of fuel was always a possibility. Especially, when we got so interested in looking for a likely spot to catch that

CATCHING THE BIG ONE

big old world record brook trout. It also includes using up a lot of fuel when detouring around bad weather.

While flying around in the late nineteen sixties and nineteen seventies, we occasionally came onto a few caches of aviation gas left there by the U.S. government when it was involved in the Dew Line Defense System with the Canadian government in the early nineteen forties. When that project got shut down, there was a variety of fuel from jet fuel, naphtha, kerosene, regular gasoline, to aviation fuel, abandoned and left to the taker. It was amazing where we found these caches of fuel. Sometimes, in the most unsuspecting places.

Depending where I purchased fuel, it was costing me up to eight dollars a gallon, which used up my pocket change in a hurry. It was like money in my pocket when my eagle-sharp eyes would spot some orange color in a clump of alder bushes or spruce trees next to a river or lake. In a matter of minutes, I would spiral down and check things out. Woe and behold, there would be a cache of fifty-five gallon drums full of 100/130 aviation fuel still sealed from the early nineteen forties. That just happened to be the same fuel I use in the seaplane.

I would mark these locations on my map for further use, as I would only take what I really needed to get us out of a pinch. For several years thereafter, I managed to have a source of free fuel, making it a little easier on my pocket. I always made sure I filtered the fuel with a felt filter similar to one used for straining maple syrup. Contaminating the seaplane's fuel system was the last thing I wanted to do.

CATCHING THE BIG ONE

The Sakami River looked very intriguing as we flew up and down the river searching for likely fishing holes or rapids. For some reason, just the looks of the river and its waters was enough to tell us this had to be worth checking out. It looked to be an ideal place to catch some of those big trophy speckled brook trout.

Down we went from the skies above to land on a section of the river where a deep hole lay just above a series of rapids. I tied the seaplane to a small spruce tree next to the rapids where we could look into the clear blue waters of the deep hole. My friends were all hepped up and so excited to go after the big trout, they didn't waste much time grabbing their fishing gear and heading downstream for some fishing. Little did they realize the huge trophy brook trout that lurked in the depths of the hole below the seaplane.

I had such a terrific headache from a long and tiring flight, I decided I would recline my pilot seat and get a bit of rest. As time went on, and the better I felt, the thought of casting a line into the waterhole beside the seaplane got my interest going. I opened one eye to take a glance at that deep waterhole once too often and decided I wasn't so tired after all.

I stepped out onto the floats to enjoy the sunshine and make a cast or two with my fishing rod, when all of a sudden, something big grabbed my lure and took off with it. Not having fished this particular river before, I had no idea what variety of fish there may be. It certainly gave me a tussle, rushing from one end of the pool to the other. When it leaped out of the water, I knew then, I had a whopper of a trout on.

CATCHING THE BIG ONE

What a beautiful trout. After finally tiring of its struggle to get free, I managed to work the trout into my waiting net. How I wished the guys were there to see this magnificent speckled brook trout. The only piece of rope I had available, was a half inch nylon rope I use to tie the seaplane with. I ran the rope through the gills of the trout and tied it to the floats to keep it alive and fresh for when my friends returned from downstream.

Not wanting to push my luck, I climbed back into the cockpit to catch some more rest. The next thing I knew, I heard a bunch of yelling from the gang, "Richard, look what we caught." They dragged me out of the cockpit to show off their catch of trout. I sort of let them carry on, not quite ready to show them what I had tied to the floats. While listening to their stories, I nonchalantly strutted around, forcefully holding back from bursting out the story about my trout. They were so happy and proud of their fishing experience, I just couldn't bring myself to interrupting them.

When the time came for them to step onto the floats, I quietly told them "see what I caught, I didn't do so bad myself." "Surprise," was the word. "Wow, where did you get that?" "Well, I'll tell you. I opened the door of the seaplane, sat down on the floats and made a couple of casts, and there it was." Using the field and stream formula for measuring the trout, "The girth squared, times the length, divided by eight hundred," the trout weighed in at a big whopping eleven pounds, thirteen ounces. Not bad!

Our agenda for the next few days involved scouting out other areas. We knew we could fall back on

CATCHING THE BIG ONE

our reserve of fuel, so we more or less had no real worries, except when bad weather appeared on the scene. We explored about every set of rapids accessible with the seaplane up and down the coastline of James Bay and Hudson Bay, and inland.

Some rivers had brook trout in the twenty to thirty inch range that were slender built and wouldn't weigh more than four or five pounds. Other rivers produced much heavier trout, due to the type of feed available. It was a good education for everyone, getting to know just where to cast our flies or lures.

When studying the rivers and rapids, we paid special attention to big boulders in the middle of the river that broke the strong rush of water and provided a quiet resting place for trout. We could almost be assured when casting into the slick surface of the water in back of a boulder, there would be a large trout waiting to grab our fly or lure. At times, we had the pleasure of seeing trout leap into the air to take the fly before it hit the water. Other excellent fishing spots were on the inside bends of a river where there may be a calm, shallow area, giving the trout a natural place to spawn.

If someone wanted a batch of trout twelve to sixteen inches in length, we sure found them. I landed the seaplane on a small lake on top of a hill and pulled up to the mouth of a small stream running out of it. We could not believe the amount of red bellied brook trout congregated in that stream. There must have been a dozen trout or so fighting to grab our lure or fly all at the same time. It was a case where we had to yank the lure away from them until we saw

CATCHING THE BIG ONE

one of the bigger ones making a rush at it and we would let him take it. It had to be a fisherman's paradise. I am sure, if someone knew how much information about places to fish I had stored in my brain, they would like to know about it.

Learning how to read the good fishing spots in a river is most important for anyone wishing to have a successful fishing trip. It reminds me of the time I took a young boy fishing. He had bought all the books he could get his hands on, on how to fish for brook trout long in advance of the trip. He figured he would have some advanced knowledge of how to catch them. Not only did he do that, but he chose to be at my side wherever I went on the river. Every cast I made, he would cast in the same spot. This, no doubt aggravated me somewhat. But, if it meant him having a good trip, and success, I refrained from telling him to keep his distance.

Once in a while, I would wait until he had a fish on and take that moment to make my way downstream as fast as possible to take a breather. The next thing I knew, he would be right at my side again. Could you guess? He ended up being the champion of the trip. Good for him! He must have had a very memorable trip, for he expressed his appreciation for several years after.

None of this could have been possible without the use of a seaplane and an experienced bush pilot. Not one river, or lake would I land on, without previously flying over it to check for rocks that very well could have put an abrupt end to my flying. Let alone my concern about those that flew with me. It's a good

CATCHING THE BIG ONE

thing I wasn't old and senile. When I decided to land in shallow areas, it was tough enough trying to remember where every rock was just under the surface of the water. In all my years of flying, I was very fortunate not to have knocked a float or two out from under me.

There was one time, when I was in the process of taking off from a large lake, the wind was kicking up some pretty big waves. I was under full power and on the step, but did not have quite enough airspeed to lift off the water yet, when I spotted a peaked boulder sticking up between the waves just in front of the left float. It was a moment of concern and elevated blood pressure, but luckily, I was able to yank the controls to the right, and back, popping the left float out of the water just in the nick of time. Otherwise, we would have had a float ripped off, or split down the middle, leaving us sitting out in the lake and taking an unwelcomed swim. It's a good thing my passengers aren't aware of a lot of these things that go on.

Sure, there is always room for a few hair raising moments, but what would life be without them. My life thrived on challenges. That's why I became a bush pilot. I feel I am quite privileged to have had the opportunity to fly in the North Country and gain such a vast knowledge of this area. I have chosen to treat the North Country, the people, and the laws of Quebec with great respect throughout my flying career.

MY FIRST
CARIBOU HUNT

Summer was slipping by while my interest in my garage business was getting less and less. During the first year as a Bush Pilot, my experience grew at a very fast pace. The long summer days spent exploring northern Canada while fishing, had given me invaluable knowledge. Having to fly in all kinds of weather conditions, such as rain, snow, fog and sudden high winds coming out of nowhere, continually put me and my 206 Cessna to the test. The more I flew, the more involved I became. My seaplane and I had become a team to challenge the north.

My first caribou hunting trip brought yet another round of adventure and thrills, but hardly in the way I expected. I had drummed up a little business to take three heavyweight football players caribou hunting. It was agreed they would meet me at Sept Isles with their hunting gear. I also arranged to meet a Canadian Game Warden friend at a lake one hundred miles north of Montreal. He and another friend would fly with me to Sept Isles to join the others.

MY FIRST CARIBOU HUNT

It was early morning as the three of us stood by the 206 Cessna, anxiously waiting for the fog to lift above the hills surrounding the lake. With a hopeful gesture, I motioned for my friends to climb aboard. The time it took for us to taxi to the opposite end of the lake, the engine would be warm enough for take-off.

As I was going through the seaplane's check list, a small opening appeared in the fog letting a little sunlight through. A glimpse up through the opening showed blue sky above. We needed an early start, as we had a long day of flying ahead of us.

Hoping the fog wouldn't close in on us before we got up through the opening, I made the decision we should go for takeoff, so pushed the throttle in to the hilt and let her rip. We managed to climb out on top of the fog where the sun was shining brightly in a clear blue sky.

As far as the eye could see, a white sea of fog lay under us, with only the highest mountain peaks showing above the fog. Most of the detailed information shown on my flight map was of little use as we winged our way towards Sept Isles. It would be at least two hours before the heat of the sun would dissipate the massive layer of fog. I had to rely mostly on my compass and sense of direction due to the lack of navigational aids that far north. Part of the time, I navigated by comparing the heights of mountain tops, to altitudes of mountains marked on my map.

As the day progressed, the fog lifted, exposing the lakes and forest below allowing me to use my flight maps to check our location with the terrain. We man-

MY FIRST CARIBOU HUNT

aged to make it the rest of the way to Sept Isles in good weather to be greeted by our other group of hunters.

The rest of the day I was very busy shuttling the gang up north to a lake in caribou country. Twelve hours of flying had left me feeling like I was floating on a cloud. When I stepped out of the seaplane for the last time that day, I found it difficult to put one foot in front of the other. It would require rest before I would get my land legs back under me.

Feeling somewhat apologetic for leaving the three men to hunt on their own. My Game Warden friend Ben, Fred and I headed north to locate the main migrating herd of caribou. We had seen several caribou swimming the lake within sight of the camp we had set up for the football players. I had given them instructions on what not to do. After all, I figured they should be big enough to take care of themselves. They should be able to fill their tags while were gone.

The further north we flew, the stronger the wind got. It was gusting far beyond the point of safe flying. Worst of all, few caribou were seen. One lone bull was seen making his way across the barren hills with no hope of getting near him. The larger lakes were so rough because of the high winds, it would have been suicide to land for fear the seaplane would break up. Previously, my head had gotten banged against the cockpit so hard, It made me see stars. I had a blister on my elbow and had worn a hole threw my jacket where it rested on the arm rest from all the bouncing around. Maybe, I should have worn a football helmet and protective clothing.

MY FIRST CARIBOU HUNT

Things just weren't looking good for our first caribou hunt. Caribou blended in so well with the moss covered ground, we were lucky to have spotted a huge trophy bull laying just over the crest of a hill out of reach of the gale force winds.

Thinking that one caribou would be better than none, I landed the seaplane in the sanctuary of a quiet cove. It was a big relief to be on the ground, as we had been bounced around enough for one day.

While my friends went their separate ways on either side of the hill where we saw the caribou, I crept on my belly towards the top. We thought, by covering three sides, we would stand a better chance of success. After crawling on my belly for several hundred feet, I poked my head up slowly to look over the top of the hill.

It was quite a sight to see. Somehow, to my surprise, three other trophy bull caribou had joined the one we had seen from the air. It was almost too good to be true. Four majestic rulers of the North lay before me, perhaps waiting for a harem of female caribou to come and join them. How I wished my two friends were with me at this moment to witness such a sight.

Slowly, I raised my rifle to my shoulder to study their antlers through my scope to see which one had the most perfect set. As the sound of my rifle echoed around the hill, all heck cut loose. The ground vibrated with the thundering of hooves as the caribou jumped to their feet and ran full tilt towards my Game Warden friend, Ben. My well placed shot seemed to have made little difference.

Bullets started striking the ground around my feet

MY FIRST CARIBOU HUNT

and whistling through the air past my head as Ben emptied his gun at the caribou.

They were directly between us and it didn't take long for me to hit the ground. I was wondering why Ben couldn't see me standing there. Evidently, he was so excited, he could see nothing but caribou. When I next glanced up, there were still four caribou on the dead run. I waited until they were clear from our line of fire and jumped to my feet and began firing.

When it was all over, three of the big bulls lay dead and the other ran straight for our friend over the hill. I could only pray that he would miss the caribou, as we could only take three.

All of a sudden, the sound of gun shots made my heart drop. Could it be, that he thought we had missed the only bull we had seen from the air. I hated to waste a caribou, and was hoping every shot would miss its mark.

Moments later, a long faced friend came walking over the hill with the sad news he had missed the caribou. I did not dare tell him how happy I felt. How little did he know we had three huge trophy bulls laying not far from where he stood. Upon seeing them, his face lit up like a Christmas tree, finding it hard to believe there were four, instead of only one.

After I had a "Hunter Safety" discussion with my Game Warden friend, we set about quartering the animals and taking pictures of the great trophy heads. We had lucked out, but the next thing, was to get back to the three men I left on a lake south of us. We ran out of daylight and was forced to camp out for the

MY FIRST CARIBOU HUNT

night before flying to Schefferville for fuel, so was given a chance to chill the meat for safe keeping on the way home.

The dispatcher at the Schefferville seabase was about the most miserable person I had ever met. He did not care much for Americans, nor did he care what kind of fuel he gave me. After three attempts to get the right type of fuel, I finally told him "thank you, I will pick out my own fuel from a stack of drums behind the building."

The first drum he gave me, had water in it. The second, had kerosene and rust. The third, had rust and regular gas. When the hassle of refueling was over and it came time to leave, I asked the dispatcher about the weather conditions south of us. He responded too quickly to satisfy me, saying, "the weather was real nice, not a storm in sight." For one reason or the other, I didn't believe him. I smelled the presence of a storm, but figured I would have to find out for myself.

We had no sooner flown beyond the first mountain range when we ran smack dab into a big snow storm that would dump thirty inches of snow on the ground. Visibility was so bad, I was forced to fly at water level following the lakes and rivers wherever possible.

Wet, heavy snow was accumulating on the windshield and the leading edge of the wings, making it almost impossible to go much farther south. The further we flew, the warmer the air got, mixing fog with the snow. When it got so bad I couldn't see the tree tops along the lake shore, I called it quits and set the seaplane down to wait it out.

MY FIRST CARIBOU HUNT

The next few hours were spent boning the caribou meat to lessen the heavy load before continuing the trip when conditions improved. I knew our three football player friends would be waiting for our return, so when the first break in the weather came, we jumped in the seaplane and headed south again, hopping from one lake to another, hoping to make it through to them.

For a while, we were able to follow a railroad that was used for shipping iron ore from Schefferville to Sept Isles, but that almost turned into a disaster. We had run into a wicked, blinding snow storm, and was flying just a few feet over the railroad tracks, when at the last split second I spotted a helicopter flying directly towards us at the same level that we were. I had to take some quick evasive action to keep from having a head on collision. Who would ever have expected to meet another aircraft on a day like that.

The visibility was down to nothing. I had to watch out for poles set up here and there along the side of the tracks. I guess the pilot of the helicopter was on the ball and made the right turn, as I did, to avoid each other. He probably was wondering who the guy was, flying a seaplane in that kind of weather.

Our fun wasn't over yet. It was not long after that, while flying through a valley that wound its way between some high mountains, a fast moving low cloud wiped out any vision I may have had. We were totally enveloped by a white mass. In an instant, vertigo had set in, completely disorientating me. With a horrifying feeling, I felt my body drench with sweat. It seemed we were diving out of control towards the ground at a

MY FIRST CARIBOU HUNT

high rate of speed.

The thought of death quickly brought me to my senses. Past experience and teaching, along with self discipline, told me to concentrate on the instruments. I yanked the controls around to bring the airplane straight and level just in the nick of time to avoid a mountain as we broke clear of the cloud. Flying, can certainly get tough sometimes, but I have learned to keep a cool head and decided not to push the bad weather situation too much.

We got stuck another three days back at the lake with our three professional football friends because of more bad weather. The North Country was setting in for its winter freeze, bringing our hunting adventures to a close.

Back at Sept Isles, a hurricane had struck while we were up north. It wiped out the docks at the sea-base and destroyed several seaplanes. I mentioned to my friends, "too bad we missed all the action."

Finding our way home was no easy task. I had a chance to practice my IFR. "I follow the railroad, I follow the river, or I follow the road." We had to deal with another storm system near Quebec City and to the west. Once again, I was forced to do some fancy low flying through the hills and valleys following railroad tracks and what dirt roads we could find.

My Game Warden friend hadn't the slightest idea where he was when we arrived at the back door of his house. I had to do a lot of what I call "flying by the seat of my pants." This was all part of bush flying, and just another learning experience during my bush flying days.

MY FIRST CARIBOU HUNT

I finished out the season by going moose hunting. Now that I had a seaplane and a little more experience, I could fly around the North Country just about anywhere I chose. Nothing much in the line of real excitement happened that last few weeks of float flying season before the lakes began to freeze over and winter set in. That was too bad, I didn't want to get rusty and lose my sharpness.

It was less expensive for me to cancel my regular insurance on the airplane and just pay for storage insurance for what little flying I might do on wheels in the winter time. I was back running the garage business full time, with the exception of a few days here and there when I would sneak off to Canada with my rifle and snowmobile chasing wolves around the hills, or taking long rides with my friends at St. Michael Des Saints.

Word had spread about my successes in hunting and fishing, and that I would fly someone north, if they wished, so I gradually built up a clientele for the coming season.

Spring could not have come sooner for me. I had already spent a lot of sleepless nights thinking of different areas to fish during the coming summer. As far as the airplane went, I knew that, from inside, out. I had laid in my bed reviewing every part of the airplane in my mind. What it did, where it was, what to look for, and what to look out for. Especially, when I get gas from some of the seaplane bases up north.

THE ADVENTURES OF A BUSH PILOT

The information center in Anchorage, Alaska with my close friends Bill and Trudy.

A forty-nine lb. king salmon caught by a client of "No See Um Lodge" that I had flown and guided in Alaska. What a trip this one was.

Another beautiful brook trout caught by my son, Richard on a real fun trip to northern Quebec.

Lake Clark, Alaska with its beautiful blue green emerald waters, so pristine and tranquill.

THE ADVENTURES OF A BUSH PILOT

Moose hunting sure gets tough at times. Too much aviation gas does a number on our clothes hung out to dry.

Just as fishing gets good, company seems to arrive in the form of a hungry grizzly.

The big one that didn't get away. An eleven pound, thirteen ounce speckled brook trout caught in northern Quebec by the author.

THE ADVENTURES
OF A BUSH PILOT

A successful moose hunt by the author and brother Wayne, and hunting buddy, Walley.

The author astride a fourteen point buck that dressed out at two hundred and seventy pounds.

Three nine to ten pound brook trout caught on yet another successful fishing trip to Canada.

THE ADVENTURES OF A BUSH PILOT

A twelve year old catches the trophy of his life. A nine and one half lb. brook trout.

The true beauty of a trophy speckled brook trout, caught by Jeff Thomas, a good friend.

The author's wife gets to go fishing as well.

A ten lb. salmon (Ouaniniche) from the headwaters of the Kaniapiskau river. These salmon have been caught in excess of twenty pounds.

FLYING FOR
THE BIG ONES

Where would you go if you wanted to go after the big ones? Northern Quebec is perhaps one of the finest areas a sportsman can fulfill his dream of catching trophy speckled brook trout. One of the best ways to make such a trip that I know of, is to find someone like myself, an experienced bush pilot with a Cessna 206 on floats and spends all season flying around the north country searching for those secret fishing holes. But of course, it is nice to have the acquaintance of two friends by the name of Ron Brooks Jr. and his father, Ron Sr., to help pay expenses. Ron Jr. and his father faithfully scheduled their vacation for mid August to go fishing in Canada.

I first met Ron and his father at a seabase, at Lake Cache, a few miles south of Chibougamou, a mining town in northern Quebec. When I first arrived, I noticed another U.S. registered seaplane parked at the dock with its occupants preparing to leave. I paid little attention, as my party and I were occupied with the task of refueling the 206. We also had to grab a

FLYING FOR THE BIG ONES

bite to eat and get our fishing permits before heading north to some of my favorite fishing holes.

At the time, the Brooks's were attempting to fly with a pilot out of New York to a fishing camp at Lake Asseneca, headwaters of the famous Broadback River. Two hours had passed before we were ready to leave, but I curiously hesitated when seeing the seaplane from New York returning.

As Ron and his father walked towards me, a look at the frustration on the face of the pilot told me there was trouble. Mildly speaking, they were upset and scared to death their pilot was going to get them killed because of his inability to fly in the North Country. He had gotten them lost several times while trying to find their way to a camp only forty minutes away.

It was quite apparent they feared for their safety. I agreed to speak with their pilot and show them the way to the camp, if he would stay in radio contact with me.

We were only minutes from the camp, when over the radio I heard their pilot's voice saying, "we are lost in a rain storm." I could only see one storm in the area, and found it hard to believe they had gotten off course far enough to get into it, when the sky was clear everywhere else.

After landing at the camp, I had to talk them in by radio while listening to their seaplane's engine off in the distance. Having to fly my own party, I could not accept a plea from Ron and his father to fly them back to New York at the end of the week. Feeling somewhat apologetic for their plight, I wished them luck, not realizing I would be hearing from them at a

FLYING FOR THE BIG ONES

later date.

My idea of enjoying the outdoors was to grab my fishing rod and camping gear, jump into my seaplane and get as far away from civilization as possible. My greatest pleasure is to catch the beautiful speckled brook trout with its bright, reddish orange belly and hundreds of small blue and purple circles with tiny red dots on its sides. Of course, we can't forget it s very distinct large square tail.

There are those that may prefer the delicacy of walleye pike for eating, but a brook trout fried in butter to a crisp golden brown makes a delicious mouth watering meal as well.

The following winter, a surprising phone call from Ron Brooks brought arrangements for us to get together for a fishing trip in August, back at the Broadback River. Ron and his father were devoted fly fishermen, strictly for the sport, and it was up to me to fly them to where they could put their skills to the test.

Though there had been a few large trout caught by others at the camp where we were staying, we found the fishing too slow to enjoy. Evidently, the water temperature was too warm that summer. It caused the majority of the big spawning trout to stay mostly in the cooler waters of the lakes.

The seaplane gave us the means to explore other areas out of reach by those at the camp. So off we flew, to check out the north branch of the Broadback River. A short time later, we were looking down on a stretch of rapids rampant with white water flowing out of a lake and emptying into a large pool downsteam. It looked too tempting to pass up, so one more convincing circle overhead, and down we went.

Thoughts of shooting the rapids for the first time in a seaplane began to flash through my mind. I studied the center of the rapids for the presence of rocks, but could only see a deep channel.

While still young and always seeking adventure, I was intrigued with new challenges. I suppose, I could have used the excuse I didn't want to leave the seaplane parked so far away from where we would be fishing, as it was a long walk down the river. Sometimes, foolish judgment is used when adding a little extra thrill or two in a day of fun. But, when you are so far away from help, it may be best to use some caution.

With all reasoning set aside, and a little nudging from Ron Sr., I nosed the seaplane into the raging current at the mouth of the rapids. By the time I felt the rushing of blood and growing excitement, it was too late to turn back. It was now up to me to keep the seaplane in the channel or we could be in big trouble.

With my fingers crossed and all hands and feet on the controls, I pushed forward on the throttle, using the power of the engine to help keep the seaplane straight. The strong current swept us downstream like a shot. Through foam and spray, we bounced about without striking a single rock.

Once through the rapids, we drifted across the quiet pool below, bringing to me the realization of the possibility of wiping out a hundred thousand dollar aircraft. That this would be my last and only stunt of this kind.

Securing the seaplane to a tree at the other end of

FLYING AFTER THE BIG ONES

the pool, reminded me of the nights I spent sleeping in the seaplane, while I let those that snored, sleep in the tent. After a horrible dream of finding myself floating down the river, I would wake up in a wicked fright, only to sit up and look out and see that I was still safely tied to the tree where I had closed my eyes earlier that evening.

There have been times when I am fishing downstream, such disastrous thoughts often come to mind. Flashing pictures of my seaplane getting loose and come floating past me. It is not a very comfortable thought, to say the least. I am always relieved when I return and find the seaplane still safely tied.

Ron and his father grabbed their fly vests and usual variety of different weight fly rods, and I, my old trusty split bamboo rod and headed for a day of fishing. It was only moments later, after several selections of flies, I was watching the graceful art of fly-fishing taking its toll, as trout after trout fell victim to the expertise of my friends. The right fly had made its mark.

It was enjoying, to see the action of Ron Jr's new Orvis rod as the line curled through the air to let the fly settle gently onto the slow moving water next to a boulder that provided a resting place for a beautiful eight pound, twelve ounce speckled brook trout.

A big splash brought a yell of excitement from Ron as the trout leaped into the air, spraying water all about, shaking its head from side to side in its fight for freedom. It raced from one corner of the river to the next, diving to the depths of the pool, hoping that some rock might cut it loose. When all its efforts

FLYING FOR THE BIG ONES

were exhausted, I readied the net while Ron worked the trophy trout within reach. Cameras clicked as Ron showed off his catch, but this was only the beginning.

A short time later, I was working the kinks out of my line while casting by a deep hole, when all of a sudden I felt a heavy tugging on my line. It was my turn to yell, bringing Ron Jr. on the run to my rescue. Everything happened so quick, he hardly had time to lower the net into the water.

In its frenzy trying to escape, the trout darted from one point of the river, to another. It was a battle between the fish and the rod, only for the fish to end up making the mistake of swimming directly into a waiting net. Seconds later, I was holding my own trophy speckled brook trout. It was an old humped back warrior that showed many battle scars. He had a large hooked jaw and half his tail was missing.

Using the formula accepted by Field and Stream, "the girth squared, times the length, divided by eight hundred," we taped the trout and came up with nine pounds six ounces. It had a girth of seventeen and one half inches.

Our luck had been good, catching two beautiful trophy trout, plus a number of smaller trout that would have opened the eyes of many fishermen. We occasionally had to deal with a few huge northern pike, where they lay quietly waiting to grab the first trout that ventured out of the safety of the faster water. I have seen five and six pound trout with big teeth marks on their body. Where they have escaped from the jaws of a northern pike, or even a big lake trout.

After all the excitement, we decided to call it a day

FLYING FOR THE BIG ONES

and head back to camp. We still had the problem of getting back up the rapids. With the gear packed and everybody aboard, I took a forlorn look up the churning waters to the lake above and pushed the throttle in to almost full bore as we fought the powerful current. This was no time for the engine to stall, as the force of the white water striking the floats bounced spray all around. One wrong slip of the rudder could have put us on the rocks that lined the channel. It was like shooting a special for an advertisement, but we managed to make it up through the rapids and onto the open lake. That concluded my shooting of rapids with my seaplane.

Another day, another river. It was Ron Sr's. turn to show us up. We flew to Lake Opotaca to scout out a small river flowing out of the west end. Making our way along the river bank, we came upon a long, narrow pool fed by a small waterfall.

The rays from the mid-day sun radiantly beamed down through the depths of the clear water where we could see the largest gathering of trophy brook trout we had ever seen. There were numerous trout in the five to nine pound range laying in the quiet of the pool, fanning the graveled bottom with their fins. It was a scene of serenity.

We were surrounded with all sorts of beautiful wild flowers that poked their fragrant blossoms up through the moss covered ground. Scattered around the hillside, an abundance of low bushed blueberries gave us delicious pickings.

Ron Sr. put his special fly on, while Ron Jr. and I sat back to watch the master at work. The only sound

FLYING FOR THE BIG ONES

to be heard, was that of tumbling water over a distant waterfall, and the slight whisper of Ron Sr's. fly line swishing through the air from his rod.

No sooner had we noticed a small ripple as the fly settled onto the surface of the mirror like water, when one of the huge trout exploded out of the water, shattering the stillness around us.

The ringing of Ron's reel told the story. Time, and time again, shock waves were sent to every corner of the pool as the trout broke the surface of the water, splashing and jumping to get free. It was like a one man show.

The scene repeated itself over and over as Ron Jr. and I hurriedly prepared our rods. We cast a hundred times, changing flies, trying everything we could, but this was Ron Sr's. day. Not a single trout would look out the corner of his eye at our fly. We should have realized we were being given a lesson by the much older and wiser Ron Sr., or was it that he was just lucky and standing in the right spot. Every time he put his fly on the water, another trout came streaking after it.

It was not until the trout stopped hitting from being spooked by all the activity did Ron Sr. lay his fly rod down to join us in a big smile of satisfaction. Few fishermen have ever witnessed such a show. I had stood by, watching a true sportsman gently release every trophy trout back to the sanctuary of the pool, to perhaps bring such a day to another happy fisherman.

Over the years, I have come to learn of many fishing holes such as this. Each one has brought a new

FLYING FOR THE BIG ONES

and exciting experience, never to be forgotten. The wonderful feeling of freedom along with its many adventures while flying into remote areas of northern Canada has brought a special meaning to my life.

WOMEN, HAVE
FUN FISHING, TOO

Becoming a bushpilot gave me great pride and joy. At times, it gave me many satisfying experiences with all the frills and glory one would want. Wherever it brought me, it brought new faces, the meeting of new friends, and many more fabulous new adventures. There always seem to be new challenges that entered into my every day life. It was impossible to duplicate any one trip, whether it was fishing, or hunting. There was always something to alter the course of events, either for better, or for worse. Mother Nature had a lot to do about that, but there again, it mattered the character of those I may be flying.

It was through a group of friends and stories of my fishing successes that two women and a grandson joined me on a fishing trip to northern Canada. It was one of those rare times that Mother Nature had provided us with the ideal summer conditions, with clear sunny days and light, gentle winds.

Our campsite, was a beautiful sandy beach on the shore of a remote lake, tucked away from the reaches of most sportsmen, mainly because they didn't know it existed. A small stand of spruce trees dotted a flat, moss covered area next to a mountain stream that emptied into the lake. Walleye pike could be caught in abundance for the serving of a delicious meal within a stone's throw of the camp.

What more could we have asked for? There were blueberries galore, and though not a very pleasant thought for the gals, we also had the company of black bear in the area. One night, one of the gals spoke up nervously, to ask, "what could have just rubbed up against the tent and her?" Not wanting to get anyone in a panic, I just told her, "it must have been the wind, nothing to be excited about."

The following morning, a scream from one of the gals standing over a set of bear tracks next to the tent, verified my thoughts of the night before. I told her, "there was nothing to worry about, he must have been just nosing around on his way to the blueberry patch."

We had a tremendous fun week. One of the ladies remarked it was second only to her African Safari trip. That was hard for me to swallow, but I thought a good compliment. But of course, it was not to be without incident. While leaving my friends at the base of a thirty five foot waterfall, I explored further upstream to find a beautiful pool where loads of speckled brook trout could be seen waiting for a new hatch of flies. I got so excited catching three to six pound brook trout every cast, in my rush to notify my friends, I paid little attention to a log straddling the brook I had crossed only moments before.

WOMEN, HAVE FUN FISHING, TOO

Hanging from under the log was a giant wasp nest. It was on my way back across the log, that the air all of a sudden became full of wasps. There must have been a million of them, hitting me from all angles. I felt like I was being kicked by a thousand mules with every sting.

My yelling didn't seem to make much difference, as I jumped and slipped at about the same time head first into the brook. The next few moments I spent slapping the mud to my head and face to help relieve the pain. By the time my friends arrived, I was hurting like I had never hurt before. You might say, I had sure disturbed the fishing hole.

The trout had congregated in a large pool under the overhanging bank, where we later came back to catch one of the prettiest batch of brookies you would ever want to see. By the way, I got revenge on the wasps by using a long stick to get rid of the nest before we did any more fishing.

It was on one of those beautiful days that week, when I flew the gang to another hot spot I knew. Previously, I had taken a twelve year old boy and his father to this spot. Before I had a chance to secure the seaplane to the shore, the boy grabbed his fishing rod and jumped off the floats.

At the mouth of the river, within a few feet of the seaplane, on his very first cast, he hooked onto a big fish. He yelled out, "dad, bring the net," but his dad thought he was only kidding. It wasn't until a large speckled brook trout made its leap out of the water, did his dad rush to help net the trout.

After the final struggle was over, the boy had his

WOMEN, HAVE FUN FISHING, TOO

trophy brook trout weighing in at a whopping nine and one half pounds. It was worth a million dollars to see the smile on the boys face. The following morning, in the same spot, his dad lands a nine pound trout.

Well, after hearing all that, the ladies were hep on fishing. As I nudged the nose of the floats against the shore, one of the gals that went by the name of Sue, grabbed her fishing rod. Perhaps, in a bit of a hurry, hoping to repeat what the boy had done, Sue stepped out onto the floats. One little slip, and she tumbled headover heals into the river, clothes and all. She came up coughing up water, sputtering and laughing all at the same time, complaining how cold the water was. Though we all felt it was quite entertaining, I thought it best to lend her a hand.

Later, we had gathered downstream at the base of a waterfall. While I was instructing Sue on how to use a spinning rod, she accidentally hit the release button. The gold lure on the end of her line dropped onto the edge of the ledge close to the rapid. Seconds later, a six pound brook trout came jumping out of the water, grabbed the lure from off the ledge by her feet and headed off downstream.

There was little question of the inexperience of the lady at the other end of the rod, but one thing for sure, she was excited to the point of jumping up and down and yelling for help. Quite a few minutes later, she hauled the big trout onto the ledge and dangled it in the air while her lady friend chased the fish with the net as though she was chasing butterflies. Even today I remark, "if it had been an experienced person holding the rod, they would have lost the fish long be-

WOMEN, HAVE FUN FISHING, TOO

fore."

I had gotten tired of watching them play with the fish, so decided to make a few casts and hooked a five pounder. As I netted my fish, I swung my net over just in the nick of time to catch Sue's trout as it fell off the hook. There I stood, with two nice trout in my net, and two really excited women jumping up and down as though they were at the Mardigras. That was one time when I really had my hands full.

It had been a fine vacation considering the experience with the wasps, people falling into the water and the excellent fishing. Of course, let us not forget the visit of the black bear.

We had a variation of fishing, including catching a forty nine inch lake trout in a small water hole in a brook one half mile up from a lake. I figured the only way it could possibly have gotten there, was during high water in the spring from all the melting of the snow.

No matter where we fished, there always seemed to be a few northern pike lurking in the edge of the fast water, adding a little extra excitement. At the lower end of the stream where it emptied into the lake, were schools of walleyes that gave us a good supply of delicious fillets for cooking over an open fire in an iron skillet and sizzling butter.

I often think of this particular trip as being one of the most enjoyable. A great therapy for a hurting soul, or for those that just need to get away. We enjoyed watching mink as they played their game of hide and seek, steal a few of our fish and disappear and when our back was turned they would be back for more.

WOMEN, HAVE FUN FISHING, TOO

At times, while we stood fishing in the rivers, otter would swim almost to us, poke their heads out of the water and give us a whistle. Several came cruising along, rolling on their backs and occasionally would come up with a nice fish in its mouth. We never seemed to be far from any wild life. There was always something new to see. Enjoying the freedom of space and the solitude of the north was such a pleasure.

I know after each trip up north I must return home at one point or another. As long as there were friends out there that wanted to go north hunting or fishing, I was ready and willing to take them.

MOOSE HUNTING
TALES

Sportsmen encounter many life threatening situations in their quest for big game. Sometimes, it can become a very wild and dangerous, life threatening ordeal. How often a completely innocent and well planned trip ends in tragedy, or happens a truly crazy experience that goes far beyond any reasonable, or logical belief. Especially, when the hunter makes his way home to the supper table and tells his story. It isn't unusual for people to wonder where he came up with such a far fetched tale. Unfortunately, some of these stories never get told because some of the originators are not here to tell them. The stories you are about to read are purely from memory of my own experiences as they happened.

It all started before I got my first airplane. I had gotten together with two of my friends (Braton and Lou) to do a little moose hunting. Our destination was a small village by the name of St. Michael Des Saints, Quebec, a hundred miles northeast of Montreal. It is considered as the last bit of civilization before jump-

MOOSE HUNTING TALES

ing off into the wilderness. We arrived there after a seven hour drive from New Hampshire.

The scene, was that of four wheel drive vehicles, cars and trucks full of hunters parading up and down the streets with moose heads tied onto the hoods or rooftops of their vehicles, and a bear or two slung across the trunk. The French language was spoken almost exclusively in the restaurants booming with business from sportsmen coming from hundreds of miles around. Indians from several Indian Reservations gathered to join in the annual Festival De La Chasse, a celebration of the moose hunting season.

Life size moose displays were erected in the yards along the streets, marking the enthusiasm of the villagers. All in all, it gave an air of excitement to three amateur moose hunters who were quite taken in with their new experience.

With such an influx of people, we were fortunate to have found a vacant motel room. The local restaurant was so busy, we had to stand in line to get a bite to eat. When arriving back at the jeep, I noticed an outfitter's business card on my windshield. There was a written message on it. "If you want to get a moose, come and see me."

Not being familiar with the area and our first time moose hunting, we pondered over the idea. It was decided we should pay a visit to the outfitter the following morning. A long drive over a narrow, twisty dirt road, and through several gates tended by gate keepers, brought us far back in the hills to the outfitter's camp.

A tall, rough and rugged looking man appeared at

MOOSE HUNTING TALES

the doorway to introduce himself. He quickly recognized the jeep as the one he had put his business card on the night before. The outfitter spoke broken English with a French accent. He was a fast talker, and it was plain to see, he was out to make some of that green stuff called American money. His face showed signs of being weatherbeaten and looked to be more half breed than anything else. We figured we would spend some time with him and see just how good the moose hunting was on his club territory.

It was early morning, clear and cold, with a light, gentle breeze blowing as we slid the big freighter canoe into the water. The five mile long lake had yet to freeze over, enabling us to paddle the long distance to the north end near the base of a high ridge. I was not aware of the fact our outfitter was taking us onto another outfitter's territory, which is a no, no. Nor did he venture to divulge any suggestion of it. Earlier, I had not seen any fresh moose sign while scouting the area surrounding the camp, so perhaps that explained the long trip across the lake.

Once at the other end of the lake, we made our way along the hillside overlooking the lake. Following our guide at a fast pace, stomping through brush and undergrowth led me to wonder if this was really moose hunting. I wondered why we weren't sneaking quietly through the woods like we normally do when we deer hunt.

The next few split seconds were spent gathering up our senses. The air exploded with the sound of a rushing freight train, drowning out any noise made by our boots tramping on the dry, brushy undergrowth. A huge bull moose had let out a blood curdling bellow that echoed throughout the woods, freezing us in our tracks.

In a fierce rage, he came charging towards us with his head lowered, knocking everything down in its path. Guns started blazing from all angles as he came closer and closer, cutting saplings off with his enormous antlers like they were match sticks. Everyone emptied their guns on him and he still kept coming.

About the time I could see his dark brown eyes rolled back in their sockets, he was only a few feet away, and showing plenty of anger. A final shot rang out, finding its mark, bringing the large animal to a thundering crash at our feet. It had been a little too close for comfort as everyone gave a big sigh of relief. We stood in wonder at the amount of lead it took to bring down this giant moose.

Our French outfitter and guide was quick to suggest we quarter the moose as soon as possible. I imagine he had his reasons, for we were on someone else's territory. This was not my idea of hunting, so we rushed the big job of cutting up the moose and carrying the heavy quarters down to the lake shore and the waiting canoe.

If we had a big load coming over, we sure had a much bigger load going back. I took the front end of the canoe and our French guide sat in the rear. My friends, Lou and Braton, straddled the moose meat stacked in the center of the canoe. It was not until we were several hundred feet from shore, did Braton tell me he couldn't swim. He was hanging on for dear life, and almost speechless. The canoe was riding so low in the water, the water was washing along his fingers locked onto the side of the gunnel. I told him, "one false move, or even the turn of your head could flip us over quicker than a wink, so unless you want to learn how to swim in a hurry, you had better play it cool."

Getting to the other end of the lake must have been like an eternity to Braton. I was well aware of the fact that exposure to the extremely cold water would have more than likely claimed our lives. The long and tedious trip back was nerve racking to say the least, as I glanced occasionally to see Braton biting his lips in sheer fright. I felt so sympathetic for him, but there was nothing I could do. Lou seem to handle things quite well under the circumstances. We had no choice, but to keep going.

As we drew close to shore, I knew very well I could not convince them to hang around for another day or two so we could try another area. It would be nice if we could get another moose or two. I guess they had enough of moose hunting, for this had not been the best of ways to introduce someone for the first time to this kind of sport.

On our way home that day, we got a surprising laugh on the outskirt of town. After thinking we were leaving all the sights and activity behind, we came upon an accident. Some hunters had tied a whole moose on top of their tiny Volkswagen Bug. It seemed their top heavy vehicle drifted off a curve and wound up on its side in the ditch. When we pulled over to give them a hand, one of the hunters was standing there scratching his bald head. I can only say, "anything goes up in this country."

Not knocking the French, because I am part French myself, but I can't help wonder at times, what happened to common sense? In my travels, I have witnessed more strange happenings. Is it because people get so enthused, or maybe I should use the words, "taken in" with their wild moments of escape to the wilds, they forget thinking twice what they are doing? Well, at least that gave us something to talk about on our six hour drive home.

MORE OF MOOSE HUNTING

Moose season can get pretty hectic in northern Quebec. Mother Nature had hit us with the meanest and roughest conditions a man wished he'd never seen. Throughout the whole month of October, sub-freezing temperatures and continuous snow storms played havoc with my flying and hunting. Three feet of snow fell over a period of three days while we struggled to keep the ice and snow off the floats and wings of the 206 Cessna. Most of the small lakes had frozen over, limiting us to landing only on the larger lakes. Worst of all, it was a bummer to be camping out in such severe conditions. After all, there is a limit to what a person calls fun.

Keeping our clothes dry and our feet warm, was a big problem in itself. We had built a fire next to the lakeshore, and draped our wet clothes over a pole straddling the fire. My seaplane was stuck solid, frozen in several inches of ice. The floats were covered with a three inch thick layer of ice. If I didn't know better, I would have said we were stuck there for the

MORE OF MOOSE HUNTING

duration of the winter. Our tent sagged with the heavy weight of wet snow, as we stood there wondering, if it was ever going to stop snowing.

With the woods being so wet with all the snow, we were having difficulty keeping the fire going. We were forced to use a little aviation gas to help it along occasionally. My friend Lou, wanted me to take a picture of him standing by the fire with the tent and the seaplane in the background. I told him, "we needed to put a little color in the picture, so throw a little aviation gas on the smoldering fire."

The next thing I knew, the quart can of gas was bottom side up over the fire. There was a big "whoosh." Flames jumped thirty feet in the air, scorching all the branches in the spruce trees next to us, including burning to a crisp all our clothes we had drying on a pole. I hadn't intended for my friend to throw the whole can of gas on the fire. I told him, "I'm glad you got plenty of color for the picture I took."

Sometimes, when all the ingredients are just right, crazy things happen. The snowstorm was finally over. A long and tedious job ensued, relieving the floats and seaplane of all the ice and snow. It was tough chipping the several inches of ice off the floats and cables. The seaplane looked like it had been in storage at the North Pole. It was necessary to cut long poles to break some of the ice on the lake so we could taxi the seaplane, as the lake was completely frozen over.

It had become a case of survival, more than a hunt. Lucky for me, I had two well disciplined hunters with me who didn't cry wolf every time things got tough. It was the last day of moose season. We were not about to give up trying to get a moose because of a little bad weather.

We hacked our way through the ice to the back side of the lake near the base of a mountain, to hopefully locate some moose. We fought our way up the hillside in snow up to our waist, climbing over fallen down trees and brush. To our amazement, we came onto deep trails in the snow, showing the telltale signs where a pack of wolves were hot in pursuit of several moose.

This was our chance. Though I knew it would be difficult for all of us to follow the tracks, we decided to toss a coin to decide who was to take the tracks. I won the tossup, and after planning some strategy, my friends Lou and Mike would work off to the sides of the tracks. We were hoping that one of us would get lucky and shoot a moose, or maybe a wolf. The question was, could we outsmart the wolves before they drove the moose clean out of the territory, or staked their claim?

Time and time again, I would circle the area, leaving the tracks to try and cut them off, but all my old hunting tricks seemed useless. Even my efforts of walking logs that were high off the ground, giving me a height advantage to help see over the deep snow and snow laden trees, backtracking and calling like a moose made no difference. I guess the wolves had them on edge too much.

The wolves managed to stay just out of sight, as though they were playing games with me. I often wondered, if perhaps I had become the hunted. May-

MORE OF MOOSE HUNTING

be, they also sensed they were the hunted, as well as being the hunter. They were in their own habitat, and would more than likely make a kill before the day was out.

It was getting late, but a stroke of luck saved the day. A bull moose had separated from the group, jumping sharply to the side of the trail around a big tree, unnoticed by the wolves. This was my chance. Now, it was just between me and the one moose. I followed its tracks through the deep snow for several hundred yards, when I spotted what appeared to be the ear of a moose sticking out from behind a tree. I thought to myself, " how could I be so lucky?"

Waiting patiently for the moose to make a move, I edged my way slowly to the right to get a better look. The next instant, the moose turned his head from behind the tree, exposing a huge rack of antlers high off the ground. With all the excitement, my heart immediately started pounding.

The pressure of being the last day of moose hunting, and expecting the pack of wolves to arrive on the scene at any moment, kept my mind on what I had to do. I slowly raised my 308 Savage to my shoulder, and with one careful shot, sent him crashing to the ground. As I walked closer to the moose, I watched the mean and angered look in the old bulls eyes as he rolled them back in their sockets.

In a struggle to get free, his huge antlers had locked under a log, trapping him where he had fallen. I watched him kicking about with his hind feet in the air, practically standing on his head. A final shot put an end to his struggle, claiming my moose to share with my two friends.

What happened after that, became a tedious job of lugging the meat out to the seaplane and staying one last night in the woods. The report I got from Lou and Mike was, the wolves had chased the remaining moose over the mountain and out of the territory.

Before we could leave for home on the following morning, it took the three of us six hours to clean the ice and snow off the seaplane. The biggest task, was to break enough ice down the lake long enough for takeoff with the load we had. Having only one camp axe and two fresh cut poles made it a difficult job. We left the wolves to their own fate, happy to have saved our own necks from becoming a victim of the savage north.

TALES OF
A BUSH PILOT

My life as a bush pilot seemed to fill my needs, in so far as making my life interesting and exciting. It didn't matter if I was flying someone moose hunting, caribou hunting, or just plain old fishing. There was always a new experience or challenge to raise a few eyebrows.

It would either be in response to one of the fellows in the party, or some crazy thing that went wrong. Like getting over anxious when we spotted a huge bull moose feeding near a beaver pond no bigger than a mud hole. A mud hole, much too small, and nearly impossible for a bush pilot to land a Cessna 206 in. That is of course, if you haven't heard of the word, "adrenalin." The biggest problem was, I just wasn't satisfied without adding a little fun to my flying. Born a hunter, and a person of adventure, put me right into another world when I climbed into the seat of my Cessna 206 and headed for northern Canada.

Hunting, had to include roughing it, so to speak. My friends and I had set up a two room plastic tent with a small wood stove made from a steel drum. It came in handy to help dry our wet clothes and keep the chill off long enough for us to crawl into our sleeping bags.

We were camped on the shore of a lake four hundred miles north of Montreal, Quebec, where I have spent many years moose hunting and knew the area well. I had certain favorite hills or ponds socked away in my memory, so all I had to do was to punch in my computer and head the seaplane for the right spot. My eyes were keen enough to spot the white marks on the head of a goose standing on the ground, so when a huge bull moose showed itself next to a beaver pond, there was little problem seeing it.

After a frosty night at camp, my hunting friends crawled slowly out of their sleeping bags and struggled into their frozen boots, while I got breakfast started over a nice hot fire. Having toast over the hot coals, with some bacon and eggs got the hunting spirit stirred up, and in a short time everyone was aboard the seaplane headed for one of my chosen hot spots.

Scattered lakes, spruce swamps, rolling hills with patches of open land, and hundreds of beaver ponds, surrounded the area we were to hunt. There were five of us in the plane, plus nearly full fuel tanks, which supposedly, limited us to the size of pond or lake we could safely land on.

All that thinking went out the window when a large bull moose and cow was seen close to a beaver pond. The nearest lake large enough to land on, was a considerable distance from the two moose. Lugging

moose meat two or three miles through thick underbrush is no easy task. But first, we had to figure how
to get the moose.

I didn't exactly have the best of hunters with me.
There was no telling what they might do to create a
problem bigger than I wished. Many times in the past,
I have passed up opportunities on getting a moose or
caribou using reasoning or common sense. This time,
my friends kept insisting that I land the seaplane in a
tiny beaver pond to put them close to where the
moose were.

We flew over the beaver pond several times at
low altitudes, studying it closely to determine if I possibly dare land. We even approached it from different
angles checking for wind conditions that might create
an unforeseen hazard. My common sense and experience told me to back off and leave this one alone,
but the adrenalin was building fast, overruling any further thinking about a decision, I would go for it.

There was little doubt it would be a tough call to
get the seaplane stopped before hitting the rocks or
trees on the other end of the pond with such a big
load. Though I tried to explain to the guys, this was
way beyond my normal call of duty, they still insisted,
"oh, you can do it."

We had one last glimpse of the huge moose just
before I stalled the seaplane over the tree tops and
flared out on the water. I immediately pushed forward
on the controls to dive the front of the floats deep into
the water to act as a brake, and even then, we luckily
just managed to get stopped about two feet from the
further shore. My friends were so "gung ho" at going

after the moose, they were totally blinded to the danger of it all. I hadn't even had the chance to tie the airplane to the shore before they were out of sight and running for the moose.

My explaining the strategy to be used made little difference, for the so-called hunters were so excited, I don't think a freight train could have slowed them down.

Well, I figured there was no sense in competing with a bunch of over anxious hunters. I took a walk upon the hill overlooking the area where we had seen the moose, thinking I would watch these city slickers do their thing. Once and a while I got a glimpse of a hunter making his way across a clearing, looking in all directions, but not a shot was heard. As I wandered over the hill further, I took notice of where the ground was torn up where the old bull moose and cow came tearing across an open stretch.

I knew better than to follow them, for they were headed out of the territory. It would be several days before they would be back. For fear of losing a hunter to the vast wilderness, miles from nowhere, I set about trying to gather them up and head back to the seaplane. Unknown to them, there was plenty of excitement left, yet.

Finally, with everyone back at the seaplane, the story of the moose chase unfolded, and of course, with no success. The next scene, was the bush pilot, yours truly, and four defeated hunters sitting on the edge of the beaver dam, wondering just how I am going to fly the seaplane out of such a small pond no bigger than a spittoon.

TALES OF A BUSH PILOT

It didn't take much thinking to realize that perhaps all of them would be making the long trek through a swamp with heavy underbrush to where there was a large lake. But first, it was up to me to fly the seaplane out of a dinky little beaver pond we had no business going into in the first place.

Somehow, we needed a little extra takeoff distance. Down at the end of the pond, several trees seem to be standing a bit too high, so we broke out the axe and shortened them up somewhat. Next, with the help of the hunters, we pulled the seaplane back into the muck and alder bushes as far as possible. Then, while two men held the tail section, I revved up the engine for takeoff. With the pond being so short, once I lifted off the water, there would be no chance to abort the takeoff.

To start with, there were three strikes against me. One, the pond was nestled down in a hole surrounded by ridges with the possibilities of down drafts that would have a big affect on takeoff. Two, the pond was way too short. Three, there was a crosswind to deal with, along with the fact that the pond was high on a mountain. I would be committed, either to make it, or crash into the trees at the end of the pond.

On my first attempt to fly out, I had the oldest of the hunters with me. I could not even get the seaplane upon the step before reaching the shore at the other end of the pond. I had to have him get out and walk with the others, if and when the time came.

It was not until the sixth attempt, that I finally lifted the seaplane off the water. In a desperate effort, I held the nose of the seaplane low over the water to gain as much speed as possible and headed straight for the base of the trees towering above the opposite end of the pond. When only a few feet from the trees, I pulled back on the controls for all I was worth, forcing the seaplane to climb straight up the face of the trees towards the sky.

As soon as the seaplane cleared the tree tops, I leveled off before it had a chance to stall. I had given instructions to my friends to take a compass bearing on the direction I flew when making a pass over their heads. That was, if I did make it out, that would be the direction they would have to walk to meet me on a large lake.

There was one relieved bush pilot as I circled above there heads, taking a straight line to a large lake a couple of miles south.

An anxious two hours passed, as I sat on the shore of the big lake, firing my rifle to signal them to the place I had landed. Five relieved and weary men gathered at the shore to recap everyone's adventure. The two men that volunteered to hold the tail section of the seaplane so I could gain a little extra advantage for takeoff, told me how they got blasted with water and mud from the blast of the propeller. They told how they hung onto the tail section as long as possible until they got blasted back into the bushes.

The walk through the swamp was tough going. They had to crawl over blowdown, through beaver dams and thick growth. After that, I decided no more small beaver ponds for the Cessna 206. It just isn't worth it.

Since that episode, when we flew over that same

beaver pond, I shake my head in wonder as to how I managed to get in and out of such a small place. I have pointed it out to several Dehaviland Beaver pilots, and they say, "no way did you go in there."

There is no question, "bush flying" has its pleasures, but with all the weather changes, it sure has its way of teaching one respect, especially, in the far north. A pilot has to be prepared to handle just about anything that is thrown at him, including snow, icing conditions, big winds, rain and fog, and people.

Most lakes generally run north and south, due to the glacial flow years ago. Southwest winds create an extra hazard for pilots because of the crosswind conditions, making it impossible to land on certain lakes when severe conditions exist. The relationship of the hills surrounding the lakes play such a big part in the action of the wind, especially on hot, gusty days, where the wind swirls around in unpredictable ways. Times that I have approached a lake that was mostly calm, where the water surface was rough, I could expect a sudden lift. Where the water was glassy in between the rough sections, there would be a downdraft. Which meant I had to be ready to push full throttle in one instant, or back off in another.

Gusty winds can flip a seaplane with a blink of an eye if the pilot isn't on his toes in these situations. Patience, and the right choice and judgment are probably the most important attributes a bush pilot could have. I have an old saying, "The old man upstairs has been riding on my shoulders throughout my flying."

As sportsman may know, quite often there are a few extra unexplained thrills, or happenings that accompany any given hunting trip. During another successful day of moose hunting, I flew my friends to an area I had seen moose earlier in the season. Landing in a narrow, shallow pond, we made our way through a swampy area heavily laden with spruce trees.

We were careful not to stir up too much commotion before poking our heads out into an opening overlooking a large bog with a small stream running through it. To our surprise, two moose were standing knee deep in muck, feeding along the edge of the stream. We were fortunate that the slight breeze was blowing towards us from the direction of the moose so they would have difficulty in picking up our scent. Two well placed shots had the two hunters their moose. That was easy, but what was to come later?

It was decided we should dress the moose as soon as possible. The day was still young, so we figured we had time to fly to another lake where some hunting friends had set up camp. We could spend some time with them and do a little story swapping. Maybe, they needed their moral boosted in case they hadn't had much luck hunting. But instead, I got involved in flying a couple of them around the area to look the territory over.

As we passed over a narrow lake at the top of the hill above the camp, we had the surprise of our life. Twelve moose stood next to a beaver house on a small point of land protruding out into the lake. Well, as you might expect, moose fever got into high gear in a hurry. There were four large bulls in the group carrying some very large antlers, increasing the tension even higher. In all my years of flying in the North

TALES OF A BUSH PILOT

Country, I had never seen such a sight. Keeping a fair distance from the lake, I circled the area, studying the lake for treacherous wind gusts and other conditions that might interfere with my landing. I had seen enough to tell me that it was not going to be a good situation.

There was no convincing my passengers that the crosswind was much too strong and dangerous for a landing, so down we went. Pulling a dead stick landing in such conditions was unheard of, but I didn't want to create a lot of noise as to disturb the moose.

Slipping the seaplane in with no power, and fighting the wicked wind gusts took about all the skill I had. We were determined to get another moose or two. Just as we touched down on the water next to where the moose were standing, they took off on the dead run, like a bunch of wild horses on the stampede, disappearing in to the woods.

Once again, I was left to tie the seaplane to the shore, while the guys anxiously headed for the woods to try for a moose. I can only say, with all the excitement generated by seeing so many moose, or in cases where hunters meet their big trophy face to face, he sometimes tends to lose his sense of wit and forgets his hunting technique, as well as respect.

And so it happens, just like the day before. How twelve large moose could avoid the hunters, I will never know. Disappointed and dejected, the men found their way back to the seaplane. We would come back later in the day when things had a chance to calm down, to try our luck again.

My next concern, was getting off the lake. The

thought of just staying put for a few hours, sounded best to me, but we were hungry and chose to go back to camp. With such fierce crosswinds blowing like it was, we would be lucky to get out of the narrow lake sitting on one of the highest hills in the area. I thought it was best to taxi to the end of the lake to study the wind conditions where we would be taking off at.

With everyone tightly strapped in, we braced ourselves as I pushed full throttle. Gust after gust lifted the seaplane off the water and slapped it back down again. I thought it was best to hold the nose of the seaplane low to build up a higher and safer speed before takeoff. As I popped the seaplane off the water I could see the sweat beads pouring from the fore-head of the man to my right in the co-pilots seat.

It would have been foolish to try climbing slowly out over the lake. I let the seaplane build its speed, while fighting the crosswinds all the way down the lake. I held the nose of the seaplane down until it seemed we were going to hit the trees at the end of the lake. I then hauled back on the control, keeping the left wing tipped into the wind and climbed straight up and out over the trees.

It had been a handful and a half, but we made it safely with a remark from my passenger as he wipes the sweat from his face, saying, "you can have this bush flying, it's not for me."

The wind finally calmed down towards the end of the day. The gang was relaxing back at camp, swapping stories of all their activities. The following day, only under better conditions, we flew back to the same lake where we previously had seen the twelve moose and managed to down two bulls before the day was over.

The next two days were spent flying the moose back to the seabase. There was one problem though. That night it snowed a couple of inches and turned very cold, freezing over the smaller lakes. When we flew back to the small lake where we got the first two moose, it was completely frozen over, posing a new danger we had not counted on.

Floats that are not amphibious do not have brakes and wheels installed on them. Therefore, short ponds and slick ice faced me with a new challenge. Hating to see two moose go to waste, I had to think this situation over very carefully. Time, and time again, I circled the pond trying to estimate the thickness of the ice and the direction of the wind. It was a decision only I could make. Wondering if I could bring the seaplane to a stop before sliding into the trees at the other end of the pond.

Keeping my fingers crossed, I slowed the seaplane to almost stall speed when coming in over the top of the spruce trees at the edge of the pond. Then, I let the floats of the seaplane gently touch the ice, hoping everything would be okay. As the weight of the seaplane settled onto the ice, the ice gave way, causing no damage to the floats, as we thankfully came to a halt.

While my two hunting partners brought the moose quarters to where I could load them into the seaplane, I taxied back and forth breaking up the ice to create an open runway. This was my first experience landing on ice, but after several trips flying in and out of the pond, I had everyone including the moose back to the main camp.

The challenge of bush flying continues to bring much enjoyment and excitement to the many that dare look for adventure and want to get way from it all. For sure, it is an escape to the freedom of the wilds. A way to capture a new look in life, or I might add, put a few extra thrills in one's life. When I fly my friends north, hunting or fishing, I try to give my all to help give them an exciting trip and best of results.

A MOOSE
HUNTING ORDEAL

Have you ever looked back over the past years and said to yourself, how lucky you are to have survived an ordeal? Well, that's what I am going to recap. An ordeal that will stick in my mind forever.

It was a clear, cold, and frosty morning in the wilds of northern Quebec. Sitting next to the shore of a lake was my Cessna 206 seaplane. Some thirty feet away, sat an old log cabin I acquired the use of for the duration of moose season. Black bear had torn out the windows and ripped down the door, but with a little work and some plastic, we managed to close off the cool, refreshing draft.

Indians from a reservation about sixty miles north had found their way by boat to this camp and swiped the stove and whatever else they could get their hands onto. We improvised by using a fifty five gallon steel drum for a stove. We cut holes in the side of the drum with an ax for a vent and a doorway to put wood through. A few stones in the bottom of the drum insulated the heat from the wooden floor. One thing

A MOOSE HUNTING ORDEAL

for sure, we weren't about to have any frost inside the cabin.

Come October, moose fever rang out throughout the Province of Quebec, and we became a part of it. This particular morning was no different than any other, when it came time to use caution and preflight my Cessna 206 before flying out for the day. But, we were all in for a big surprise.

Stepping from the doorway of the log cabin, my friend and his eighteen year old son approached with buckets to help wash the heavy coat of frost from the airplane, while I did my usual inspection. The first big surprise, was to find the seaplane's battery flatter than a pancake. Propping a three hundred horsepower, six cylinder engine under freezing conditions is not the easiest thing to do, as most pilots will attest to.

There was a feeling of confidence to see the seaplane well secured tail first to a tree on shore with a half inch nylon rope. After giving my friend Tinker instructions on how to work the throttle, I made my way to the front of the seaplane. I was standing in the lake with the water up to the top of my hip boots while trying to prop start the engine.

It was an awkward situation. A lot of uncomfortable thoughts raced through my mind. There I stood, up to my rear in water in front of a seaplane, cranking on the prop. What if the engine started and the rope didn't hold, or I didn't get a chance to jump into the cockpit in time to grab the controls before something drastic happened?

Without life in the battery, we could not use the

A MOOSE HUNTING ORDEAL

radio to call for help. Worse yet, Tinker, to whom I gave instructions, was sitting at the controls in the cockpit and knew nothing about flying a seaplane.

My continuous efforts of pulling on the propeller quickly put large blisters on my hands, but I could not give up. After repeatedly priming the engine manually and resetting the controls, the engine finally roared to life. I yelled to Tinker at the controls to slow the engine down by pulling back on the throttle, but in his nervousness and excitement, he instead, pushed the throttle control all the way to the dash, to full throttle.

All three hundred horse power was pulling for all its worth on the one rope anchoring the seaplane to a tree. Though the rope was stretched to its limit, it was holding the seaplane from certain destruction. I scrambled out of the lake as fast as my legs would let me, and rushed around the tail of the seaplane. I had to get at the controls to slow the engine speed down. I looked up just in time to see Tinker's son, Roger, holding an axe high over his head, ready to cut the rope. Luckily, I got to Roger just in time to yell. "Don't cut that rope." It could have been a fatal blow. We would have been standing there watching both his father and my seaplane headed for doomsday.

A few hectic moments passed before all was under control. Tinker was still sitting in the cockpit, and in such a state of panic and shock, he nearly had a heart attack. As he stepped out of the seaplane, he was cursing and muttering something about forgetting all about my instructions. No one can explain what possessed his son Roger to think he should cut the rope. How lucky for us, he didn't.

A MOOSE HUNTING ORDEAL

The rest of the hunt went fairly smooth, with only minor problems. I had taken Tinker and Roger up on the side of a hill that was heavily wooded with spruce trees. We picked up the tracks of an old bull moose and hadn't followed it but a short distance before the animal jumped up in front of us. When the shooting was over, and the moose had run his last few hundred feet through the woods, there were congratulations and cheers.

Later in the week, we had to fly to a seabase to get fuel at four dollars a gallon, and returned back to camp just before dark. Unfortunately, there was water in the fuel. Come the next morning, after another cold night, more trouble showed up. I had found the reason for the battery being flat. Back at the first seabase we stopped at, the mechanic had accidentally stepped on one of the battery cables with his size twelve shoe while checking the engine compartment, shorting out one of the cables.

While taxiing the seaplane, I made sure I gave the engine plenty of time to warm the oil and do my run-up, I noticed the engine did not have the necessary fuel pressure for takeoff. Further inspection found the fuel system and strainer bowl to be full of ice. Just enough fuel was getting through to run the engine under low power. If I had attempted to take off without a proper check, we would have crashed.

Wherever I have flown, it has been my experience to be extra cautious. I always double check any maintenance that my aircraft receives. Perhaps, that is why I am still around to write these tales of a bush pilot.

CARIBOU HUNT
AND THE PARTRIDGE

It was an early September morning, when I met a friend of mine by the name of John Roberts from Canaan, NH, along with a friend of his by the name of Al. We had met at a dock on Lake Sunapee belonging to my brother, Wayne. We were standing by my Cessna 206 on floats, checking out our gear stacked on the dock in preparation for a caribou trip. Our destination was northern Quebec, close to the Labrador border, and nearly a thousand miles away.

It was necessary to take with us the proper equipment that would allow us to survive for a few days in case of an emergency, or bad weather. It included a tent, axe, sleeping bags, rifle, and ammunition, plenty of food and the proper clothing.

Loading a seaplane is an art that only the bush pilot fully understands. It was most important for me to pack the heavy items, such as extra fuel toward the middle of the cockpit, or center of gravity. The lighter

CARIBOU HUNT AND THE PARTRIDGE

items of baggage were packed in the rear. Cameras and lunches were the last to go in the seaplane. They were put on top within easy reach.

The sun was just rising over the hills east of the lake which helped in dissipating the white, grayish fog from the lakes and valleys. With a last minute check of the weather conditions along our route and some quick good-byes, we climbed into the Cessna. John rode shotgun in the copilot seat, and his friend Larry, sat in the seat behind him.

With a last wave of good-bye, we taxied away from the dock, taking time to warm up the engine and to the necessary procedural magneto check, oil pressure, manifold pressure, along with a few other visual checks. Moments later, the 206 Cessna lifted into the air as we smiled with joy and anticipation of heading north.

As we flew towards the Canadian border, we found ourselves over a massive blanket of fog. Somewhere under that blanket of fog, was the Connecticut River. It stretched from northern New Hampshire, all the way to the ocean by the state of Connecticut. Though we couldn't see the river, I knew it was under us, because of flying this route plenty of times in the past.

There were valleys rich in farm land that lay at the foot of the mountains overlooking the river. But today, all we could see was the mountain peaks towering up out of the white shroud that hid the beautiful landscape below, or perhaps a small beaver pond tucked away high on a mountain side.

It was a beautiful morning with a light westerly

CARIBOU HUNT AND THE PARTRIDGE

breeze, giving us smooth flying. By the time we arrived between the hills by Lake Willoughboy in northern Vermont, the fog had pretty well dissipated. Soon after, we were looking down on Lake Memphremagog where we land to clear Canadian Customs. Our flight would then take us by Sherbrook and on past Quebec City, to follow the St. Lawrence River as far as Sept Isles. After refueling at Sept Isles, we would fly northward to a lake next to the Labrador border, just south of Schefferville.

Flying at fifty feet over the St. Lawrence river was quite eventful. We watched hundreds of white whales swimming about, while huge black whales surfaced like submarines, shooting their big water spouts high in the air. There were also hundreds of seals laying along the sand bars. As we flew close by them, most seemed to get up and scamper into the water. We encountered flock after flock of beautiful white snow geese and the regular Canadian geese on their way south for the winter.

There were thousands of ducks in large groups scattered along the river. Sometimes, they could be seen in protected coves, or at the mouths of small rivers that flowed into the St. Lawrence. It was their regular annual event of migrating south to mark the coming of winter. Also, bringing near the end of flying season for those that flew their seaplanes into the North Country.

Occasionally, we would make the trip more interesting by flying past the deck of a freighter transporting supplies down the river, and see the crew standing on deck waving to us.

CARIBOU HUNT AND THE PARTRIDGE

Not all of the trips north have been as nice as this day, for I have encountered many stormy conditions that required setting down on a lake or river. At times, that lake may be out in the wilderness, or with luck, we would find a handy beach near a cottage where the inhabitants were very hospitable.

Our last stop to get aviation gas was at Sept Isles, where we hastily topped off the tanks, got our caribou permits and headed to our final destination, "Lac Fleur DeMay." In English, it stands for "May Flower Lake."

It was late in the day when we arrived at "Lac Fleur De May." We set about the task of setting up camp, putting up the tent, building a fireplace, and puffing up our down sleeping bags for the night.

Later, while sitting around the camp fire eating a few fresh cooked brook trout and toasted bread, I took the liberty of telling some of my wild and crazy hunting and fishing stories.

The next morning brought another fine day with John and Larry still reminiscing over the stories I had told them. We had discussed our plans for the day, for what was to be their first caribou hunt and experience in the North Country.

John had his hip boots on and his Remington 270 slung under his arm. Larry, toted a 30-06, and I, carried my trusty Zebco spinning rod in one hand and my 308 Savage in the other. The reason for the spinning rod, I had been here before and discovered a small pond over the ridge loaded with sixteen to eighteen inch red trout.

As we walked along the edge of a ridge looking

CARIBOU HUNT AND THE PARTRIDGE

for caribou, a partridge flew up from by our feet and landed in a small spruce tree a few yards away. I quickly put up my hand and told the men "stop, don't make a move, I am going to catch us a partridge for supper." John spoke up and said, "what are you going to catch it with?" I said, "my fishing pole, what else?" He laughed and said, "I have got to see this. I have never heard of such a thing."

I handed John my 308 Savage and took steady aim with my trusty Zebco spinning rod. I let drive a daredevil lure at the head of the partridge, just missing its head by about two inches and got caught on a branch above it. Not wanting to scare the bird, I told John and his friend, "stay still, I have an idea."

Stepping slowly forward several feet, I let the fishing line dangle in front of its beak. Then, I twisted the line in my fingers to form a small loop. As I worked the loop slowly over the head of the partridge, the line rested on its eye lid, causing it to blink. The partridge probably thought it was just a fly, so continued sitting on the branch, unaware of what I was up to.

As soon as I got the loop over its neck, I yanked on the line, trapping the partridge from flying off, and quickly ran up and grabbed it. My ten pound test line held it fast. We had our partridge for stew, but what to do with it while we hunted, was the next concern.

I decided to carry the partridge back to camp for safe keeping. While carrying it by the neck about six hundred yards to the camp, I realized the bird was still alive. I remarked to my friends, "if this old bird is so determined to live, I guess I will let it go." Holding the partridge in my hands, I threw it into the air. The

CARIBOU HUNT AND THE PARTRIDGE

partridge flew off and landed in a distant tree, alive and well. I know, some fellows I tell this story to, tell me they should have worn their hip boots, but this is a true story, I swear.

Well, after that episode, we set off over the ridge again to find some caribou. We ate wild blueberries from the bushes scattered around the hillside, while our eyes were busy searching the open terrain for one of those big trophy bulls that so often seem to appear out of nowhere. Sure enough, a large bull carrying an enormous set of horns was spotted feeding in a marsh at the end of a lake.

Larry, was to have the first shot, so I instructed him to keep low to the ground and get behind a small mound of dirt. I watched the caribou while Larry got in position. Finally, I heard Larry's rifle report and saw the big bull go down, but only for a few moments and he was back on his feet. The second shot knocked it down for good and everyone ran over to admire the trophy bull with a rack to be proud of. Congratulations were in order, and then, the job of quartering the animal and getting it back to camp.

Larry was absolutely mystified because he couldn't find where his first bullet hit the caribou. I jokingly told him the first bullet must have just come so close, the caribou must have laid down in fright. Larry was absolutely certain he had to have hit the animal twice, but yet, where? Well, you never would have believed it. The caribou was standing with his rear end toward Larry, looking over his shoulder at us. It appears, that Larry shot a little low, cutting the testicles clean off the caribou. With the sudden shock of it all, it knocked the caribou flatter than a pancake...now you know the rest of the story.

The day was not quite over, so I took John and Larry to the pond to show them what else I could catch with my trusty Zebco fishing rod, besides a partridge. We made our way along the shore, staying just high enough upon the bank so as not to spook some of the prettiest brookies my friends had ever laid eyes on.

There were trout with bright red bellies, fat as can be, fanning their fins on their spawning beds within inches of the shore. Some trout spooked real easy, while others would dart under the overhanging bushes when we came too close. Seeing as how I only had my one and only trusty spinning rod that I carry in the seaplane at all times, I offered to share it with the others. We alternated using the rod, giving each person five casts at a time.

With all the activity, no one could possibly have gotten bored. Trout were going in all directions. I carry a few flies to use with my spinning rod as well as lures, but when we used certain flies, the trout would rip them to pieces on us. They fought so furious, with the bushes being so close to the water's edge, we had a problem landing them. We had to fling them through the air over our heads and onto the bank.

Every cast we made with the fly on the end of the spinning line, there were a dozen trout fighting to hit it all at the same time. We didn't have the action of a fly rod, but the end results were very satisfying. With all the activity, the guys forgot all about caribou hunting.

Mother Nature had taken her special paint brushes out when she painted the red trout with so much beauty. We caught several measuring eighteen inches in length and they were fatter than a ball of butter. They were added to our collection of several others laid out on the moss. John and Larry took turns catching fish and when we figured we had enough for supper, plus a few to take home, we headed back to camp.

After cooking up a few trout in butter to a nice golden brown with a little salt and pepper added, along with some home fries, it was time for everyone to retire for the night. Well, as you know, a bush pilot, along with acting as a guide, needs his rest, so I elected to sleep in the airplane on a foam mattress, out of the way of those who snore so loud, it makes the tent shake.

During the night, I heard the pitter patter of small feet on the floats of my airplane. I sat up and looked out the side window. Standing on the floats, a slim shinning black coat glittered in the moonlight with four little feet and a bushy tail. It was a mink, staring up at me with his little beady eyes.

I didn't think too much of it that night, being tired from a hard day, but come morning, my thoughts were confirmed. All those beautiful red bellied trout came up missing. I had packed them in moss in a plastic bag and buried them in the beach by the rear of the seaplane to keep cool and safe. "Hah!"

Well, it seemed like Mr. mink had called in all of his relatives for a nice feast on my brook trout. I was saving them to take home to my mother. They had totally cleaned out every last one of the trout that

CARIBOU HUNT AND THE PARTRIDGE

night. I felt angered in a way, but I figured all the more power to them. The next day, we were so busy caribou hunting, there was no time to catch any more.

John had shot his caribou a long way from camp. The easiest way to haul it back was to fly the seaplane to a lake close to it. The lake we chose to land on was very shallow for several hundred feet from shore. Not expecting to run into this situation, I left my hip boots at camp. "Always take your hip boots with you, no matter what," I tell my friends.

Because I could only get the seaplane within a couple of hundred yards from shore, John was forced to giving me a piggy-back ride. It seemed strange to see the seaplane sitting high in the water out in the middle of the lake, grounded. Needless to say, it was quite a chore carrying the caribou meat out to the seaplane.

After a big struggle pushing the seaplane around to face into the wind, we managed to power it into deep water. With the benefit of the waves helping the seaplane skip along the surface of the water, we made our exit and flew back to camp.

When packing up to head home, it always gave me a strange feeling, almost like I didn't want to go. But I knew, if we dragged our heels much, we could get socked in by bad weather with the blink of an eye. John and Larry had a very memorable trip, and it was up to me to get them home. They surely will have plenty of stories to tell.

RESCUE OF
LOST HUNTERS

Throughout my years as a bush pilot, I have seen numerous occasions of hunters getting lost, or fishermen getting into the worst predicaments. Sometimes, it is not without choice, and sometimes it may be a case of bad timing. There are those that prefer to have booze the larger part of their grocery list when on a hunting or fishing trip. It may even be the case, where the gang is so "gung ho," they perhaps let their ambitions over ride their capabilities and forget common sense. Either way, it has spelled disaster, and brings big problems for many sportsmen.

But, on rare occasions, some are fortunate to be saved by a stroke of luck. While flying around the wilds of northern Canada in my Cessna 206 floatplane, it has been mostly the good luck and good fortune for some, that a caring and concerned bush pilot just happened to be in the right area at the right time.

During moose season, I had set up camp at the north end of a twenty mile lake. With the possibility of other hunters being in the area, and not wanting to

RESCUE OF LOST HUNTERS

interfere with them, my friends and I flew to the south end of the lake to see if other hunters were camped on the lake. As we approached a camp site, I noticed a written message of "help" on top of the tent.

A big burly fellow frantically ran from the tent waving his red hat, motioning to us for help. I explained to my friends. "we should land and see what their problem is, and offer a hand if necessary."

One of the hunters had been lost for three days. All their efforts to flag down other seaplanes flying by, was to no avail. The big fellow, a French Italian from Montreal, sobbed profusely as he told his story. They pleaded for us to help find their partner and to call out the Royal Mounted Police and Game Wardens. It took a while for me to calm them down.

I discovered they had only one compass between the four of them. Either it didn't work, or they didn't know how to use it. I could not speak enough French to understand all that they had to say, but I volunteered to help find their friend.

My friends stayed at the camp while one of the French speaking fellows flew with me in search of there partner. He was trying his best to communicate with me, hopefully to give me the right directions as to where he thought they were when his friend got lost. It was like getting a lesson in sign language and looking for a needle in a hay stack.

A hectic search ensued. For an hour and a half, we flew over every bog, pond, lake shore, and ridge, hoping to spot some form of human life.

My French passenger was in a state of hysterics, saying. "It's a hopeless search and a lost cause. I just

RESCUE OF LOST HUNTERS

know my partner is dead." As difficult as it was to communicate, I tried my best to console him. Through my own perseverance, and a last hopeful effort, I flew way beyond the area the lost hunter was believed to be.

It must have been fate, for I spotted the hunter on the edge of a small grass bog, waving his hat wildly, trying to catch our attention. My French friend jumped with joy at the sight of his partner, and whatever he was saying, I am sure it was alright. I put the seaplane into a steep dive and turned the seaplane on its side as we passed low over his head, motioning I would be back.

We made a quick return to camp, then stripped everything from inside the seaplane's cockpit to reduce all the weight possible, including all the seats, except mine. I would need every bit of performance I could get out of the 206.

The nearest place I could land to the lost hunter, was a small pond divided by a sand bar. I had to land in one part of the pond and bounce the seaplane over the sand bar onto the other. Then, I pushed forward on the controls to cause the front of the floats to dive deep into the water to act as a brake, hoping to get stopped before hitting the trees at the end of the pond. It was a little hairy, but my Cessna 206 and I were a good team when it came to situations such as this.

It was necessary for me to go deep into the woods to rescue our lost hunter. It was only after repeated attempts of firing several shots from our rifles to signal one another before finally meeting up with him.

RESCUE OF LOST HUNTERS

He was one very happy man when we stepped foot on the shore of the pond and saw the seaplane sitting there.

He was surprisingly in good shape for not having eaten in several days. But needless to say, he was very relieved to have been rescued from almost certain death. We were able to communicate with each other, as he spoke English well. I felt it was necessary for him to understand he was in for a hairy ride out of the pond, as I explained what I had to do about hopping over the sand bar and all. He told me, "no airplane ride could compare with what I have just gone through, so don't worry about me."

With all my senses set for peak performance, I pushed the throttle full open. Just as we approached the sandbar, I yanked quickly back on the controls, skipping the seaplane over the sand bar and onto the next body of water. I then held the nose of the seaplane down to gain all the speed possible before popping it off the water for the second time.

For a few moments, it was touch and go when I had to tip the airplane's wings vertically to go around the corner of the pond and stay between the ridges while climbing up and out, narrowly clearing the trees and hills. With the grace of God, we managed to make it safely back to camp. My passenger had taken it all in stride, considering his last few days in the woods.

A reunion of four big, rugged looking, but sensitive French Italians took place up on our arrival. Tears of happiness and the emotional stress poured from their eyes. The men embraced each other and then shook

RESCUE OF LOST HUNTERS

my hand in appreciation for my help. By this time, I was beginning to get involved emotionally, myself. I am sure they will remember this moment for quite some time.

Later, while stopping at my friends seabase, I was thanked again, for it had been their party of hunters that I had rescued. I did get my fuel tanks filled for free, but it was not my intention to be rewarded in that way. It had been reward enough just to know the good feeling of helping someone survive to join their loved ones.

As I bounce from one story to another, it brings to mind of another incident where some of these professed hunters just don't pay attention to where they are going through the woods, or how to get back to the particular spot where they entered the woods.

How little did a moose hunter realize his plight, until I arrived on the scene at days end. There he sat, enjoying a tasty snowshoe rabbit by the comforts of an outdoor fire on the shore of a Canadian Lake.

Earlier that day, we had seen a large bull moose and a cow feeding in a river. They were only a short distance, perhaps several hundred yards from the lake where I dropped the hunter and his partner off. I agreed to let them go it alone to pursue their quest, assuming they couldn't possibly get lost in such a small area. Plus, they would feel better in their new experience.

I gave them all the necessary instructions, making sure they had the proper compass bearing and how to approach the moose without scaring them. They were left some emergency supplies and their sleep-

RESCUE OF LOST HUNTERS

ing bags, just in case I didn't make it back because of bad weather, or whatever. It would also give me a chance to check on other friends camped on lakes elsewhere.

I must mention, not once have I flown away from dropping off a party of hunters without being concerned for their safety, or something going wrong. I have had too much experience to have total trust or belief in hunters when they tell me not to worry when they say they are quite capable of being on their own, and used to the woods.

It was mid afternoon when I approached the spot where I had last seen the two hunters. Nowhere could they be found. Perhaps they were sitting by the river where they were to have killed the moose. I flew low over the river for miles in either direction, but found no hunters. Nor could I see any sign of a moose being quartered.

Finally, I spotted one of the hunters on the far end of the lake where I was to meet them. Upon landing, a very excited man tells me he had lost contact with his partner shortly after leaving the lake. He never did get to the river, for he had floundered around in the woods all day, fighting his way through alder bushes and swamp, luckily to have made it out. Any time a hunter pokes his head into the bush, it is not without risk of some sort.

We climbed into the seaplane to anxiously search every inch of the area. We flew over every bog, river and lake, keeping a sharp eye out. It seemed impossible that we should have missed spotting the red clothes of our missing hunter.

RESCUE OF LOST HUNTERS

The day was quickly coming to a close as darkness began to settle in. Our hopes were dwindling fast. In one last effort, I flew further to other lakes far beyond our normal search pattern. A puff of smoke was seen rising from by a small cove surrounded by spruce trees, tucked back away from the lakeshore.

As I made a low pass within eye level, I did not concern myself as to disturbing who it might be by the fire. To our big surprise, we were looking into the face of our lost hunter. He was sitting there enjoying a rabbit dinner.

As we stepped out of the seaplane, we were greeted by a happy, contented hunter, wanting to know what kept us. Would you believe, he actually thought he was on the same lake I had dropped him off at, earlier that day.

As we recapped the day's events, the look on his face changed to total surprise when the reality of his mistake set in. It was like he became frightened to think of what could have happened, and so thankful to have been found. He told me, "I never reached the river, but instead, I got tangled in a thick alder swamp and came face to face with a gigantic bull moose. I didn't dare shoot it, for fear it would charge me."

The only way he could have come out to the lake where he did, was to have gone parallel to the river. Many times, similar cases like this happen, but some hunters are not so fortunate to be found.

On another occasion, two brothers got the urge to go moose hunting in northern Quebec. Snow storms plagued the north country on a daily basis. We would spend hours flying through blinding snowstorms, or make big detours in an attempt to get to my favorite hunting area.

There were times when we were totally consumed by turbulent snow squalls, making it altogether too dangerous to fly, forcing us to turn south to get out of the storm and onto the safety of a lake.

When we eventually were able to reach our destination at the north end of a large lake, we set up camp near a series of beaver dams that provided good habitat for moose. I figured to have a nice, easy hunt for the rest of the day. I gave instructions to my friends so they hopefully wouldn't get lost, but for some reason, hunters don't seem to pay much attention.

One of the hunters stayed in my company, while his brother supposedly did what he was instructed to, but that wasn't altogether true. He had gotten involved chasing several moose, forgetting where he was. He followed the moose clear out of the territory, not to be seen the rest of that day, or night.

I flew around the area trying my best to locate him before darkness overtook me, but it was not to be. I am sure the man missed the comforts of the tent and his sleeping bag that night.

There was little doubt the night was any shorter for him, than us. All I knew was, I had my hands full, trying to console his brother.

The night was spent pondering over questions of where he was. "was he still alive?" "How did he go wrong when I gave him such clear instructions?"

Daylight found us back in the air, searching every beaver pond or bog, hoping he would know enough to head for a clearing. A threat of snow was in the air, and it had been very cold. Much too cold to be spending the night in the woods without a sleeping bag. We had to find him, or he would be a goner.

We extended the search further and further away from where he should have been. The thought of him being dead were becoming more of a reality. If he were alive, why wasn't he near a lake or clearing? I had circled high above the hilltops to give him a chance to see us and to let him know we were looking for him.

Luckily, through determination and instinct, I flew over a lake, which was half a days walk from the camp. Next to a tiny cove, I saw a small puff of smoke rising up through the spruce trees. It was only by making a closer inspection did we know we had found our lost hunter. After landing and taxiing into the cove, we saw a man jumping with joy, but with the look of a man who thought he would never see his family again.

He had burned half the forest down trying to keep warm that night. I told him, "the next time you plan on staying out, you had better take your sleeping bag with you."

Tears of deep feelings between the two brothers ran freely down their faces. They were so relieved to be together again. It was like I could see the sign in their eyes, telling the possibility of what could have happened, and so happy it didn't.

On our way home, the story unfolded about how he chased five moose over the mountain and forgetting to keep track of his direction, or the time of

RESCUE OF LOST HUNTERS

day it was.

Perhaps we could say, this was one moose hunting experience they would prefer to forget.

With all the hunting I have done, and with so many people, it usually is only a matter of time before I run into another situation where a hunter has to do the wrong thing. I had taken a couple of acquaintances moose hunting. Seeing as how moose like to hang around rivers, we decided to taxi the seaplane down a particular river to look for that elusive big bull moose.

After a few hours, we were to meet back at the river's edge where I parked the seaplane. But, when the day dragged on and one person came up missing, the hunters companion and I became quite concerned. Darkness was setting in. We were supposed to fly into civilization for the night to a little logging village called Parent about three hundred miles north of Montreal. It was difficult to believe anyone could get lost hunting near a river.

In desperation, I jumped into the seaplane to take a look around. Just maybe, I could spot our friend somewhere out there. As it turned out, we found our friend several miles downstream. He had followed the river in the wrong direction, if you can believe that.

I nosed the seaplane up to the bank and shut the engine down just long enough to hopefully have our lost hunter jump onto the floats. We were pushing darkness, and patience was short. By this time, the current from the fast moving water was drifting the seaplane back away from the bank of the river. I kept yelling to our friend to jump onto the floats. "Hurry up,

RESCUE OF LOST HUNTERS

it's getting late, jump." In his frustration, he forgot to put a little "ump" in his jump and ended up landing in the river. I saw his gun barrel pop up out of the water, then him. The water was quite deep at that point, but we grabbed a hold of him and dragged him onto the float.

With his clothes wringing wet, he climbed into the seaplane for a wet and cold ride into Parent with darkness on our heels.

As though we didn't have enough to contend with, when we arrived at the seabase, we were greeted by three plain clothes game wardens. We were asked if it was okay to check inside the seaplane. I said, " sure, help yourself." Unaware to me, our lost friend had not unloaded his rifle in all his excitement. When one of the game wardens checked his gun out and found it to be loaded, all heck cut loose. They impounded my seaplane, took my friend off to jail, and took his rifle.

I had to do some fast talking to a friend of mine in Montreal who was in charge of the game wardens in order to get my seaplane released. I don't know why it is, but it always seems that people with a little authority have to let it go to their head. It was a totally unintended mistake. My friend did end up losing his four hundred and fifty dollar rifle. So much for that. I just thought I would throw this one in.

THREE MOOSE HUNTERS LOSE THEIR LIVES

There were three business men that hired the services of a seabase at Chibougamou, Quebec, a small town in northern Canada. They were flown to a lake to spend a week of moose hunting. The very same day they were dropped off with all their camping gear and canoe they anxiously set out across the lake to hunt on the other side.

Big winds whipped up huge waves, making their trip extra dangerous. Thoughts of safety were soon left behind. Their life was snuffed out in a matter of moments. Their canoe had tipped over, drowning two of them, while the other supposedly lucky hunter, managed to swim to a tiny island of rocks in the middle of the lake. A few days later, he was found frozen to death with a knapsack over his head, hoping to keep warm. It was a great loss to their loved ones and to their community. I have often thought, how I wished I had been around to come to their rescue.

LUCKY
SURVIVORS
OF A DOWNED
AIRCRAFT

It was on a trip to northern Quebec, several hundred miles from civilization. The day was hot, with the temperature well into the nineties. I was flying at an altitude of about thirty five hundred feet when I looked down to see a seaplane sitting in a precarious position on a bend in a river. One float was partly in a river and the other was sitting high on the beach.

The river was too full of rocks to believe the pilot had intended to land there unless something drastic had gone wrong. We saw several people standing beside a tent, making me wonder if perhaps they really were in trouble.

I alerted my friends on board that I was going to spiral down to get a closer look. When passing low over the downed aircraft, it was quite apparent the pi-

LUCKY SURVIVORS OF A DOWNED AIRCRAFT

lot had engine problems and had to ditch the seaplane among the rocks in the river.

Everyone seemed to be content and happy, not giving me any sign to come to their rescue, so I assumed the pilot had notified someone for help on his two-way radio.

Upon reaching a seabase later that day, I inquired as to anyone knowing about a downed aircraft. A quick telephone call to the Department of Transportation acknowledged, that indeed there was, but it was several hundred miles north of the location of the crash site I marked on my flight map. After more discussion, it was determined that the pilot had given them the wrong information as to their whereabouts. I gave them the exact location, and a helicopter was sent to their rescue.

Several days later, upon returning to the seabase, I received a message of thanks from the Department of Transport, as well as from the occupants of the downed aircraft. How lucky for them, I just happen to be flying over and take an interest in their plight. I guess it is my nature to be curious when I see something out of the ordinary. Or perhaps it is a way for me to return the kindness so many others have given me.

BOOZE TAKES ITS
TOLL
ON HUNTERS

A lone, sad, moose hunter waits in hysterics for a seaplane to arrive from a seabase a hundred miles away. It was at the end of the week and a seaplane was supposed to pick up, what was supposed to be, he, and his three friends.

The first few hours in camp had been full of celebration. The four hunters were on their annual moose hunt. They had brought plenty of booze with them to enjoy their stay. We of course, have witnessed many situations where one has had one too many, but mixing booze with fishing, or hunting in particular, has never set too well in any group. I was thankful not to have been involved with this horror story, but I was in the area at the time and could not help but be concerned.

It seemed, that the week started off with too much drinking, and ending up with one hunter being shot by accident. Another hunter lost his life while getting

BOOZE TAKES ITS TOLL ON HUNTERS

lost. The third hunter, unfortunately tipped over in his canoe and drowned. It was without a doubt, a terrifying week for the lone survivor, let alone their loved ones at home. I always tell those that wish to fly with me, if drinking is what they want to do, look for someone else to spend their fishing or hunting week with.

There was a time, when I arrived at a camp in northern Canada for a quiet week of fishing, that I had to play doctor. I was greeted at the dock by several sportsmen in quite a frenzy. Their friend had fallen over the railing of the deck, face first into the bushes and dirt, wedging sticks and dirt into his eyes.

I asked, "had he been drinking?" The look on their faces was enough. "Some," the remark came. It was too late in the day to be flying anyone over a hundred miles to a doctor. I suggested the fellow collect himself and lie down on a bunk. I would see what I could do. An hour of careful work probing in his eyes with clean tissues, I finally brought relief to the hurting soul, grateful of someone having steady hands and patience.

On another occasion, a fair skinned, heavy set fisherman demanded he be flown to the nearest hospital. His face and ears were slightly swollen due to a few black fly bites. The whole camp was on edge wondering what to do with this man. Well, "Doctor Richard," (yours truly,) arrives on the scene, just as darkness was setting in. I am not thrilled about flying through pitch black in a seaplane, especially in the north country where bad weather can come up at a moments notice, or if I had to land on a lake, I couldn't see where the rocks were.

BOOZE TAKES ITS TOLL ON HUNTERS

A quick inspection of the man told me all he really needed was a good hot soaking in the shower. The following day, nothing more was said.

ALASKA BOUND

It was early June, nineteen eighty four, when fate tipped its hand in bringing to reality my long life's dream. My wife had given me a choice, "either go to Alaska, or I will divorce you." That left me with little recourse.

Divorce, or not, the thought of living my dreams of going to Alaska seemed the best of choices. I don't think it really would have mattered what the consequences would have brought. Perhaps, a break from all the tension at home was just what the doctor ordered, if you know what I mean.

I've heard tell, Alaska is the last Frontier, and I sure as heck intend to see what its all about before I walk my last mile.

Alaska, is a land full of wild life and adventure, along with its many challenges to the best of men. In fact, according to some of the stories I've been told by those that have been there, I can almost be guaranteed a few unexpected thrills of my own. Especially, where there's an abundance of grizzly bears. If the sight of one of those huge bruins charging upright doesn't cause your hair to stand up in a hurry and the blood rush to your head, I don't know what else will.

ALASKA BOUND

It doesn't seem to matter, whether your at one of your lucky fishing holes, or camped out on the shore of some beautiful, majestic lake with its glittering blue green emerald water from a glacier high up on the mountain. You don't want to argue with a grizzly when he feels its time to eat. It just might be "his" lucky fishing hole as well.

In these instances, the smartest thing to do, is to make a quick, quiet retreat to a safe distance until the bear has had his fill. I always figured, when you see the hair standing up on the back of a grizzly's neck, you don't want to mess around with him unless you have a three hundred magnum at your side.

The fishing in Alaska, speaks for itself. With the annual run of the huge king salmon, the sockeyes, pinks, and many other species of fish, it gives the sportsmen all the fishing they want, including some fantastic rainbow fishing.

I was sure to be treated with the sight of caribou herds migrating over the tundra, and the occasional giant moose feeding at some of the small ponds scattered thereabout with their huge antlers always ready to ward off an attack from a pack of wolves.

For years, I had been wanting to go to Alaska, and now, I had the opportunity. Previous conversations with an outfitter had virtually guaranteed me a job using my seaplane to help fly his clients to remote rivers, salmon fishing.

The months of June and July, are prime times for the king salmon to make their annual spawning runs up their chosen rivers. This follows spending several years of their young lives growing up in the ocean.

ALASKA BOUND

Conditions at home hadn't been very rosy, so between the threat of being shoved out the door, and the chance to go to Alaska, I chose the latter.

Several days of planning was necessary for the trip. It required several telephone calls to Canada to locate a total of thirty seven flight maps to get me from New Hampshire, across Canadian territory, and into Alaska. Needless to say, it was necessary to purchase a larger brief case for that amount of maps.

Courses had to be plotted. Navigation and communication frequencies searched out and listed, as well as calculating distance and flying time between fuel stops. The majority of flight maps necessary for the trip were of Canadian territory, requiring me to procure them from the Department of Lands and Mines, Ottawa, Canada. Also, there was a list of equipment and clothing needed. Such as extra fuel, sleeping bags, tent, and emergency supplies.

By now, I was far from being a "green horn", as the saying goes. Sixteen years of flying the "bush" in northern Quebec had earned me the rank of an accomplished bush pilot. The vast amount of experience I had acquired, logging several thousand hours in my 206 Cessna would surely be a great asset to help insure a safer trip to Alaska.

A search for someone to accompany me and to help defray expenses, was surprisingly easy. The biggest problem, was bad weather. It persisted from the east coast of Canada, to the far west, causing several days delay in our departure date. Rain, snow, and fog menaced our entire flight path.

I was being pressed for time as I was to be at the

ALASKA BOUND

outfitters, "No-See-Um Lodge," located on the Kvi-chak River by mid June for the arrival of his clients. My many years of flying experience wisely told me to use caution and not get this trip off to a bad start.

The following morning, a final check on the weather brought us good news. The stormy conditions were breaking up and we could prepare to head out on that long awaited trip to Alaska.

Belford Richards, a close friend of mine, agreed to fly with me and help pay expenses. His medium build and light weight would be a big help, as it would give us the opportunity to carry some extra fuel. He also, is a person that seems always open for new adventure. It makes for a much better trip flying such a distance with someone you know, of which I was very thankful.

Belford had visions of panning gold nuggets, and maybe even staking a claim on some old abandoned gold mine. He brought his video camera to document the events of the trip and some of the fantastic scenery along the way. Luckily, Belford had previously loaned his gold dredging equipment to a friend already in Alaska, as we would not had the room to carry it in the seaplane.

On the morning of departure, I was given the bums rush out the door by my wife who couldn't wait for me to leave, and arrived at Lake Sunapee with baggage in hand. My brother Wayne, gets all the prestige for allowing me to park my seaplane at his dock, but I shouldn't mind, I get away from having to pay the high lakefront property taxes.

As I walked onto the dock, Belford was waiting

ALASKA BOUND

with his camera running, and to my surprise, tells me we have another passenger. His tall, and very attractive blonde wife, Joyce, was standing beside him all decked out with high heeled shoes and all.

I thought he was joking, until I noticed he had brought two sleeping bags instead of one, as well as extra suit cases. This presented a new problem I hadn't counted on. As it was, we were running close to the seaplane's gross weight, which meant something not quite so necessary for the trip had to be unloaded to make room for Joyce and her luggage. Belford insisted I knew his wife was going, so I quickly dropped the subject, glad to have her aboard.

Joyce was not what you'd call a country girl. She was raised in Ohio among city folks. Perhaps, that is why she appeared dressed for a queen's ball, with plenty of makeup, long finger nails and all. I quietly kept my thoughts to myself. I knew she would learn to come better prepared next time when flying over five thousand miles of wilderness. There is always a good possibility of camping out on some remote lake for a night or two.

Luggage had to be packed according to the center of gravity. Extra fuel was stored on board, along with a supply of emergency food and survival gear. Joyce was assigned the seat in back of the co-pilot's seat occupied by Belford. His job, was to aid me with the many flight maps I would use for navigation. Little did I realize how much of the five thousand mile trip would be made flying by the seat of our britches, mainly due to bad weather.

As we taxied slowly away from the dock, my broth-

ALASKA BOUND

er and his wife standing amidst the stack of discarded baggage waived their good-byes. It was an envious waive. The look in their eyes was enough to tell me how badly they wished they were making the trip. Our family is close, and when one or the other does something special, the others share their feelings.

Moments later, though we were loaded to the hilt, plus always that little bit more, my 206 was making its way down the lake, fighting to lift its heavy load into the air. Not until the floats of the seaplane had broken free from the vacuum of the water, did the seaplane eventually lift off. Our eyes turned back in the direction of my brother and his wife to get that last memorable look, knowing full well it would be two months before we would see them again.

The expressed excitement in our voices indicated only too clearly how happy we were to be on our way. The deep, "gutty" sound of the seaplane's engine brought music to our ears as we climbed slowly upward to watch the shores of Lake Sunapee disappear behind us. I could now put my thoughts on what lie ahead. This would be a first for me and my seaplane, flying from the state of New Hampshire, to Alaska, and on to the Bering Sea.

We followed a course of two hundred and ninety degrees over the rolling hills of Vermont, and across the upper state of New York.

Some two hours into the flight, found us circling over the Canadian Customs located on the St. Lawrence River, in the area known as the Thousand Islands. Mirror like conditions on the water reflected perfectly the many trees that shadowed the river's

ALASKA BOUND

edge. Its serenity only reminded me the summer season had not yet begun. The few boats on the river presented little problem as I brought the airplane in for a smooth landing on the slick, slow moving surface.

At the dock provided by the Canadian Customs, Joyce stepped to the cockpit door, looking for a hand down. By the expression on her face, and being in high heeled shoes, I could see she was feeling quite insecure. I am sure the thought of swapping them for something more comfortable and safer was weighing heavy on her mind. I quickly rushed to her aid, for having someone slip and hurt themselves is the last thing we needed. Belford stepped from the seaplane as we were greeted by the Customs agent, who with a curious, but usually kind and unapprehensive way, was quite surprised to hear of our destination. After a few moments of close scrutiny, and a wish of good luck, we were soon on our way.

Belford and Joyce were enjoying the trip, amazed at the ease and fun dropping onto just about any body of water we chose. This was only the beginning of a long flight, and already Belford was busy with his video camera, capturing the scenes surrounding our stop.

After clearing Customs, we climbed slowly up and over the river, giving us a chance to view the many Islands and summer cottages surrounded by fresh, deep green spring foliage. The summer season was not quite upon us so we didn't see all the hustle bustle of boats darting here and there and water skiers streaking from one point to another. It reminded me of

ALASKA BOUND

me of the quiet times after Labor Day.

Joyce was already looking for the next stop, wherever that may be, hoping to replace those high heeled shoes of hers. It was a little difficult to drop in on main street with a seaplane. I kindly told her, "perhaps the next stop may be more convenient." As this was our first look at this part of the country, we had no idea what was in store for us. Like it, or not, we would have to take things as they come.

We continued on course, passing just to the east of Lake Ontario. The terrain was that of scattered lakes and low land, heavily wooded, with only the occasional village. Beaver dams dotted the wilderness, providing moose with plenty of natural habitat.

Flying at low altitudes allowed us the opportunity to see huge bull moose with their antlers in full velvet, majestically standing guard over newly born calves and their mothers. Other forms of wildlife, such as black bear, geese and ducks, were seen foraging for food amongst the spring's new vegetation. We could even see the round, circling ripples appearing on the surface of some of the smaller ponds, indicating the many brook trout feeding on a new hatch of flies.

It was late in the day when we arrived at Wa Wa, Ontario, a small town on the northeast corner of Lake Superior. It has been my experience to avoid having to park my airplane at a large lake due to the danger of big winds, which could wreak havoc to it. Consequently, I chose to land on a lake overlooking the town nestled between high mountains. I managed to locate a safe place near a public picnic area where we could secure the seaplane for the night.

ALASKA BOUND

A two mile walk to town convinced Joyce more than ever to seek the first shoe store open. There wasn't much to see in the small town of Wa Wa, but Belford was following up the rear with his video camera capturing the few points of interests. Wherever we went, the locals found little difficulty in picking out the strangers that had arrived. It seemed, as soon as we landed the seaplane anywhere near a town, word would spread like wildfire. Perhaps, the unusual sight of a seaplane arriving with strangers may have something to do with it.

Joyce managed to purchase not only one pair of shoes, but an extra pair. She was happy to pack away her high heeled shoes and rush to a motel to nurse her sore, aching feet. After a long day, we were in dire need of a good hot meal, to be followed by a long nights sleep.

The following morning brought problems of where to get fuel for the seaplane. According to the recently dated flight map, there was suppose to be a seaplane base on the lake where we landed. The motel manager said it was out of business, but he could arrange with a friend to help get fuel from the local airport. An airport that always seems to be so far out of town. The extra fuel we left on the dock back home to make room for Belford's wife would have come in handy.

This was only the first of many scheduled fuel stops. If this was to set an example of what was to come, I could see it as being a major problem. After several trips to the airport by car, and the use of several gas cans, we finally got the seaplane refueled and ready to go. We would soon learn that there would be many more delays, much beyond my control.

The town of Wa Wa was swallowed up in the brilliance of the early morning sun's rays as we made our way out over the deep blue waters of beautiful Lake Superior. Ledges towered straight up, high above the northern shores of the lake. Spruce trees decorated the ledges, glistening with their new spring growth.

To the south and west, far beyond where the eye could see, stretched a massive body of water. Mother Nature had presented us with its very best of days, not a cloud in the sky, with clear visibility to the horizon. Because of the good weather, I chose to fly directly across the northern tip of the lake to save fuel and time.

We flew for quite some time over nothing but blue, open water. It must have been close to an hour and a half before we spotted land and a few scattered islands on the western shore of Lake Superior. We were so involved enjoying the flight, I hardly noticed a familiar calmness that surrounded us. Glassy water had replaced the ripples and waves seen earlier. I had seen this many times before and it could only mean one thing.

Just beyond the lake shore, a gray cloud mass confirmed my suspicions. Within minutes, our beautiful day had come to an abrupt end. I hadn't totally believed the weather report I got from the airport that morning. I was told the weather was clear for several hundred miles. Maybe he was talking about the local area around Wa Wa.

I soon found myself busy with my flight map, flying

ALASKA BOUND

at treetop level, through rain and fog, trying to make it to civilization. At one point I was sure we were within ten miles of a highway leading into a town, but was forced to do a one eighty due to fog and visibility.

Thoughts of spending the night in a comfortable motel was on my mind, and try as I did, all my efforts to get to civilization failed. Sticking our necks out any further, was beyond my better judgment. There were lakes and small ponds in the area, but only a few large enough to take off from. We had little choice, as by now, the fog had gotten so thick, I barely could see the lake under us.

Once on the water, the seaplane was completely shrouded in fog with the shoreline totally obscured. It was useless to study the map to pick out the lake we were at, until the weather cleared. One thing certain, we were not within walking distance of the comforts of a motel.

Moments later, we were quite surprised to see the bow of a boat appear out of the thick fog making its way in our direction. All I could think of, it had to be some hardy, inquisitive fisherman wanting to help us from our plight. After a brief conversation with the fisherman, we followed him back through the fog to a camp site on shore. We soon learned the name of the lake to be "Muskeg", well known for its northern pike fishing, and what we were to experience in the next twenty-four hours, I don't believe any of us will ever forget.

Joyce was still in her best of dress, and tenting out in the mud and rain back in the "boonies" didn't seem very appetizing. We elected to ask the fishermen the whereabouts of a motel, and if perhaps they would be interested in taking us to it. The answer was "yes, that it was approximately thirty five miles."

Though things seemed okay, my senses were telling me to keep my guard up. It was finally agreed, we would go for the motel idea. We had to trust someone. After all, it wasn't all that far, according to what we were told.

After speaking with some other fishermen camped nearby, they agreed to watch the seaplane in our absence. We secured the seaplane safely for the night, and followed the two fishermen to their van. As we stepped inside the van, the stench of liquor was so overwhelming, it almost gagged me. In fact, it reminded me of one of the rankest odors I had ever smelled while visiting a little Mexican town called "Tijuana." Camping gear was strewn everywhere. It looked like a bear had gotten in their van and had a ball.

It was tough acting the part of a supposedly rugged outdoorsman and bush pilot, not ever having had a drink of liquor. Before my dad died, he used to tell me, "you may not like the situation your in, or who you are dealing with, just carry on and smile like there was nothing wrong." That philosophy has kept me out of trouble a few times. A quick glance at Belford and Joyce acknowledged that they didn't like the situation any better than I did.

The driver leaned over the rear seat tempting to rouse a third person. I saw a head pop up, only to crash back onto the floor with a thud and groan. When the driver saw me give him a questioning look, he responded by telling me, "my friend gets that way quite often when he drinks a little too much tequila." That explained the wicked odor. Bottles were strewn from one end of the vehicle to the other. They sure must have had a party for themselves. I wonder how they enjoyed their fishing. My gut feeling was crying within, that perhaps it would have been better if we had stayed by the seaplane and slept in the tent. I could vision someone breaking into the seaplane and stealing all our luggage. Regardless of our concerns, we decided to put everything in the hands of the man upstairs and get on our way.

The several days of rain had caused the old logging road to be slick and muddy. Not knowing how much drinking our driver had done, we could only hope for the best while we kept our fingers crossed under the seat. We bounced in and out of ditches, over boulders, around and over logs, and hit about every pot hole there was. The way we slid about, one would think we were on an African Safari, or traveling over the back lands of Australia. I kept glancing at my watch to have an idea on travel time and distance, but if the motel was only thirty five miles away from the lake, it must have burned down, or gotten swallowed up in some mud hole.

It was difficult to keep a conversation with the driver, and not many answers were being given. Finally, it was like a god send, a main highway loomed up in front of us. A slight hesitation from the driver led me to wonder, does this guy really know what he is doing, or is he guessing just where a motel might be?

I know, tequila crazes the mind, but what was our next step. As far as I could calculate, we were headed due east, exactly back towards the direction we had flown from, earlier that morning.

The driver was resting his foot heavy on the throttle, with the speedometer needle ranging from speeds of sixty to ninety miles an hour. Thoughts were flashing through my mind. Could this be the way I am to die, riding with some wild guy with too much liquor under his belt? Why was it, that I survived so many years of high speed motorcycle road racing and snowmobile racing, let alone the thousands of hours I flew as a bush pilot through all kinds of weather?

Finally, after what seemed like hours of driving, we came to a road sign, indicating Thunder Bay, Ontario. We had come all the way back to the shores of Lake Superior. I hoped we would make better progress the following day. Beyond a junction in the road, sitting high upon a bank, was an old rundown motel. According to the way our driver spoke with the owner of the motel, it appeared they knew each other, but whatever the case, and much to our relief, we got our motel, such as it was.

There was little chance for further discussion with our driver before he yelled from the van, "I'll be back in the morning to pick you up," and he was gone.

The old rundown motel cost us one hundred and twenty dollars for the night. Though it was a pleasure to sleep in bed, compared to camping out in the rain and muck back at the lake, if I had my own transportation, I believe I would have looked for better accommodations further down the road.

We found the menu to be on the short side, as the only food available, was a coke and a hamburger.

ALASKA BOUND

That cost us seven or eight dollars each. It was quite a let down, considering what we had in mind, like a nice well cooked steak. This guy must have thought he had a monopoly on the food business. There wasn't another restaurant for miles around. We'd have to make up for it at our next stop.

Come early morning, the sky had a deep, dark overcast, accompanied by scattered fog. According to the weather news, it was to clear for later in the day. I couldn't believe my eyes when our chauffeur drove up, minus his two companions. Believe it, or not, he was sober and walking a straight line. He seemed to be in a big tear to take us back to Muskeg Lake, which suited us just fine.

I spent most of the night worrying about my seaplane, wondering if those outlaws cleaned us out. I didn't dare look in the back of the van to see who else might be there. It cost over a hundred dollars for the ride, to and from the motel, but the ride back to the lake was a little more gentle than the day before.

Muskeg Lake was apparently well noted for its northern pike fishing, and attracted a wide variety of sportsmen. We were only too happy to see the weather clearing and the remaining fog burn off, giving us a clear look at the lake. It was only then, that I could see the lake was long enough to take off with our heavy load.

The several fishermen camped next to the lake, were wringing out their wet clothes and packing up to go home, while I was preparing for take off. All I can say is, we would have been flat broke long before we reached Alaska, if each stop cost as much as this one did. After a very late start, it was mid afternoon when we finally bid farewell to Lake Muskeg. We had been in the air only a few short minutes when we found ourselves flying over highway seventeen, the road I so persistently tried to reach the day before. We had used up a lot of fuel flying around in the storm, forcing us to make an unscheduled fuel stop. Hopefully, it would not be too far away from our present location, and near our flight path.

It is amazing how much fuel gets gobbled up on the slightest deviation from a plotted course. According to the flight map and the airplane's fuel gauges, we had enough fuel to make it to Eagle River, near Dryden, Ontario. According to the map, we should be able to get fuel there.

We had lost most of the day because of a late start, but within a short time, we were circling above Eagle River and North Shore Lodge. There was no choice, but to land and take our chances, hoping we could arrange to refuel the seaplane. I didn't realize we were going to be stopping at a very swank, high class lodge.

As we were directed to a long dock, we could see a beautiful lodge constructed of logs with large glass windows overlooking the lake. Smaller cabins were nestled among spruce trees above the main lodge on immaculately kept grounds. To accommodate some of the more fortunate clients that vacation at the lodge, a grass air strip had been conveniently carved out of the forest adjacent to the cabins. The owner, personally escorted us on a tour of the area, which naturally had to include a bit of airplane talk, follow-

ALASKA BOUND

ed by an invitation to stay for the night, our third night of the trip. Belford was once again bringing his video camera into action taking pictures of the lodge and surroundings, including the staff.

Getting fuel the following morning turned out to be a bigger problem than anticipated. I was led to an old antique fuel pump dated back in the early nineteen hundreds. "There she is." the owner said. "It hasn't been used in a couple of years, but I have plenty of tools in the shed."

The desperation for fuel made me more determined than ever. Thankful for my mechanical skills, but not for the time lost, I managed to get the pump working, and was soon about the task of lugging cans of fuel to the seaplane. Once again, precious time was lost on our schedule to get to Alaska.

The hospitality shown at North Shore Lodge was a delightful experience, and to be highly recommended. Shortly after a good hearty breakfast of bacon and eggs with home fries, we said our good-byes, to continue on our long journey. This stop had been quite a contrast, compared to that at Muskeg Lake and its drunken fishermen.

For a change, it was smooth flying for the next one hundred and sixty eight miles to Selkirk, just north of Winnipeg, Manitoba. Our flight path took us across the southern tip of Winnipeg lake, about three hundred miles in length. Less than half an hours flight later, we crossed Manitoba lake which was part of a chain of lakes that spread northward for another three hundred miles.

ALASKA BOUND

There was no shortage of Provincial Parks in the area of our flight path, but being so early, everything looked deserted. The countryside had flattened out considerably, with the exception of an occasional hill. There was an abundance of lakes and rivers that gave us a sense of security and let us breath easier in case of engine problems. Also, to our favor, the further west we flew, the longer the daylight hours became, enabling us to get in more hours of flying.

By now, we were getting well into Manitoba. We had gotten an early start for a change. The wind had subsided and it was a nice clear day for flying. Working our way over desolate, uninhabited hard to navigate territory, with a combination of map reading and instrument flying, we managed to put behind us a full day of flying.

Joyce had finally settled down to whatever might crop up in our daily encounters of flying. I have to chuckle when I think about that statement. Oh well, such is flying. It actually was nice to have her along, as she was good company, as well as helped prepare the sandwiches or snacks, while I kept busy at the controls.

Belford was still at it with his video camera, taking pictures of anything that looked interesting. He did an excellent job capturing my expression while I was concentrating on my flying. He forgot to shut off the camera when he laid it in his lap while the lens was pointing directly at my face. When we reviewed the film later, we were surprised to see that. I often wonder, if only there was a way I could see beyond the horizon. Perhaps I would be in a better position not

ALASKA BOUND

to depend on so many inaccurate weather forecasts. It is unfortunate when one wishes to fly, there are so many elements that have to be dealt with. Some of those, are the availability of fuel, the problem of visibility and wind. The following experience is a good example of some of these elements.

After flying for quite some time under relaxed and most enjoyable conditions, isolated industrial cities and mining towns appeared out of nowhere. It was at one of these such towns I was forced to land due to severe winds and heavy rain. The only seaplane base for miles around was just below us, and being lashed by gigantic waves.

The mountains we passed over a few miles back reminded me of the horizon I spoke about earlier. On one side the weather was beautiful, while the other was like a monster, attacking us with everything it could throw at us. It was next to impossible, and stupid of me to think I could safely land near the seabase under such rough conditions. We had come too far to risk damaging the seaplane, let alone our lives.

Fierce, powerful winds beat us about like we were a toy seaplane, putting the maximum test to the wings as I searched anxiously for the safety of a protected cove. All my experience was being called upon. The only possible safe place to land was at the northwest corner of the lake where it was partially sheltered from the winds.

Belford and Joyce tightened their seat belts sensing it could be a rough ride down. It was a tough and tiring flight. My hands were just about paralyzed from fighting the controls for such a long time. But after a rough descent in hurricane like winds, I was able to bring the seaplane safely down onto the pounding waves.

As luck would have it, I found the shoreline to be too rocky and shallow, preventing us from getting on shore and having a safe place to tie down the seaplane. Rather than take the chance of damaging the floats on the rocks, I was left with no other option, but to try and make our way to the seaplane base.

Having to taxi parallel to the huge waves only added more danger for fear of being capsized. This was one time I was thankful for the heavy load we were carrying. It helped to stabilize the seaplane, making it more difficult for the wind to blow us over. As it was, we were being tossed about like a cork in the middle of an ocean.

The silence in the cockpit was broken time and time again by the crashing of high waves and tor-rential rain against the windshield and fuselage. At times, there were sharp, whacking sounds, "kawack" when the rotating propeller would suddenly get inundated with a huge wave.

Progress was slow, and at times, I had to shut the engine down to keep the water spray from ruining the propeller. I would then sail the seaplane backwards, using the rudder to control the seaplane while the wind blew us down the lake. By repeating this process, I was able to keep the nose more into the wind with less chance of us being blown over and losing everything we owned. Belford and Joyce were very quiet, but I will bet they were taking in the whole situation.

ALASKA BOUND

After what seemed to be an eternity of life on the edge, it was a great relief when we finally managed to reach the seaplane base. Several pilots had been standing helplessly by, watching our ordeal, waiting to help secure my seaplane. They told us the weather had kept them shut down all day, and was surprised to see us arrive.

That was one day, I can honestly say, I had enough flying. We would have to stay the night in the local motel. There was at least one bit of good news. According to the weather forecast, the following day was to be clear. "Yeah, an early start."

I would like to add, that no matter what the circumstance, I have found the Canadians to be very hospitable and friendly, especially when it comes to pilots helping one another.

The following morning, blue skies and bright sun brought a welcomed surprise. The pilots at the seaplane base had a heavy schedule to make up for lost time, and we had a little making up to keep our own schedule. The wind had subsided substantially during the night, bringing us a happy relief. After giving the seaplane a thorough going over, I felt we should take advantage of the good flying conditions and make an early departure.

Crossing Lesser Slave Lake and working our way over desolate territory, we managed to get in a full day of flying. A combination of map reading and instrument flying got us through uninhabited wilderness country that was hard to navigate. At this point of the trip, we had managed to get through the Province of Manitoba. When we see all the desolate country flying from one end of Canada to the other, it makes us wonder why people pay such big money to live next to a city. At the moment, there seems to be plenty of land to build on. I guess it may be a question of how far out a person wishes to live.

Nipawin, Saskatchewan is a small town out in no man's land. It is supported by a hydro power dam on the Saskatchewan River that lay just ahead of us. About thirteen hours of solid flying brought us over the river at the north end of town where I had scheduled a fuel stop. It was late in the evening and had been a long, tiring day. We could see only one lone seaplane tied to the river's edge. There were no gas pumps, or fuel drums visible up and down the river.

Here we go again. Once more, the new maps I had purchased from Ottawa, Canada, supposedly up to date, let me down. This was getting to be a pain in the butt. There was no other aviation gas available for hundreds of miles.

After landing on the deserted river, I taxied downstream, looking for someone to tell us where we could get some fuel. Or perhaps, we could find a spot close to town to park the seaplane. Maybe, with a little bit of luck, we might find a motel.

All of a sudden, two men came speeding down the river in a boat. I waived frantically to get their attention, but all they did, was to come racing by us and head back upstream.

The last few minutes of daylight was quickly fading away, leaving us little time. I was determined to talk to them. I pushed the throttle to the dash and had the seaplane skimming across the surface of the water in full chase. We caught them just in time to hail them down as they were driving off with their boat already loaded on the trailer.

The driver, reluctantly got out of his truck to talk to me. For a moment, I thought I was seeing Robert Redford. Here was a guy stone drunk, and a perfect double for a movie star. He had hit a rock in the river and smashed a hole in the bottom of the boat, not daring to stop earlier, for fear of sinking. "Climb into the truck," he commanded. "I'll help you out one way or another."

This guy was sure in a hurry, I told him, "give us a few minutes while we hastily secure and lock the seaplane." He kept reminding us of his drunken state. Not only verbally, but with his driving. I told our newly found friend who looked so much like Robert Redford, we needed fuel for the seaplane, and also a motel for the night. He remarked about the seaplane base as being a thing of the past, but mentioned, perhaps if we were lucky, we might be able to get fuel from an old abandoned airport a few miles out of town.

In his effort to contact a person to do with the abandoned airport, we had the ride of our life. He was all over the road, driving over curbs, narrowly missing mail boxes and lamp posts.

He backed into streets in front of oncoming traffic and whatever, at speeds that seemed like sixty miles an hour. Perhaps it wouldn't have been so bad, if he hadn't been towing a large boat.

I desperately, but politely pleaded with this guy to just let us off at the closest motel, but he wouldn't hear of it. He kept insisting that we stay at his house.

ALASKA BOUND

He offered to let us use his truck for the night and told us to leave it wherever we wanted to, he would find it the next day.

He was so drunk, I didn't know if he really knew what he was doing. If the truck had been in better condition, I may have considered his offer. The muffler was broken off, the fenders hanging, and the windshield broken. And by the way, half of the truck's running lights were out as well.

He told us, "before they got any law in town, I could drive drunk all over the place and do what I wanted to, but nowadays, I have to be a little more careful." He couldn't prove it by me.

Never before had I felt so close to death, as we were being driven ninety miles an hour across an old steel bridge with left and right angled corners on it. I had to keep looking back to see if the boat was still behind us. At one point or two, I didn't think there was enough clearance for my fingers to fit between the truck and the bridge.

After the wild and hair raising ride to his ranch, our Robert Redford look alike didn't have to ask again to convince us to stay the night. Considering what we had endured during the past hour, we were quite content not to venture any further.

It was not until we were formerly introduced to his wife, did we get to know them as the Mitchells. Though our host was a bit out of it and feeling little pain, our evening was quite enjoyable, as well as entertaining. We were served sandwiches and other refreshments, while our host was putting the black coffee to him trying to sober up before going to work at

ALASKA BOUND

five A.M. He was employed at the power dam on the Saskatchewan River.

Belford and Joyce were having fun trying to coax our camera shy hosts into being captured on video. We tried, unsuccessfully I may add, to convince our new friend Mr. Mitchell he should go to Hollywood and apply for a job as a double for Robert Redford. I think by his actions, he preferred to stay in Nipawin where he could do his own thing. While speaking with Mrs. Mitchell, I was quite surprised to hear that she too, occasionally indulges in a wild drinking spree. I promptly let the discussion drop.

With all the activity, time had slipped by. When I glanced at the clock on the wall, it was three A.M., making it a long day for three very exhausted people. It was like music to my ears when someone suggested it was time to turn in. Everyone had told enough stories and jokes for one night. To top it off, we were given an invitation to stay over on our way back from Alaska. We politely remarked, "we would have to think about that one."

My life as a bush pilot has been anything but dull. Surviving the normal every day routine of bush flying has its own share of adventure and challenges. At times, it's the unexpected and unknown that can really liven up a bush pilot's life in a hurry. Whatever the case, flying has been very enjoyable for me, partly because of the interesting people I meet.

It had been a short night. What little sleep we did get was well appreciated. Up to this point of the trip, we were spared the inconvenience of sleeping out in the tent at some remote lake. Most of the people

ALASKA BOUND

we had come in contact with, have been very helpful.

Our brief stay at Nipawin turned out to be happier than expected. Arrangements for fuel were made with a local airport mechanic. Mrs. Mitchell transported us between the old abandoned airport and the seaplane during the procedure of refueling, hauling fuel in five gallon gas cans until the job was completed.

Mrs. Mitchell was a great help. Her husband had somehow managed to drag himself out of bed long before we did, in order to get to work on time. We thanked her kindly for all their help, as we shoved off on the next leg of our trip.

Four long days had passed since leaving home. Mother Nature had thrown just about everything she could at us, causing exceptional delays. At times, either strong headwinds, or rain and fog slowed our progress substantially. So much bad weather had set our schedule back by almost two days. Now that it was staying light until close to midnight, if all went well, we could make it to British Columbia by the end of the day. I decided to make use of the daylight hours to make up for lost time.

Saskatchewan, with its many lakes and Provincial Parks, had been most interesting and very beautiful. But, as we got over Alberta Province, it became quite a different story. We found ourselves flying over wild, desolate country with very few lakes to land on in case of an emergency. Short, scrubby trees covered the terrain with its many petite rolling hills, while the glittering water of scattered beaver ponds could be seen throughout the countryside.

As we continued on, there was a stretch or two

where we were kept well occupied when seeing an abundance of moose, black bear, and elk. I wondered, if perhaps we were flying over a wildlife preserve, seeing so much game.

There was no civilization in sight. The sooner we got to an area where there were more lakes, the better we would feel. I didn't relish the thought of trying to land in a beaver dam that was no bigger than a bath tub. The terrain in the western part of Canada was quite different, compared to that I was used to in northern Quebec.

By late afternoon, we were flying over farm country with miles and miles of crop land. The only water in sight was that of a large river winding its way through a gorge several hundred feet deep with its walls leading straight up from the river's edge. It was like the river had carved a twisting path in the earth over thousands of years. According to my map, all we had to do was follow the river straight into British Columbia.

We must have flown close to an hour following the gorge, when the huge Rocky Mountains were seen towering high above the horizon. British Columbia was just ahead.

I swung wide of Fort St. John and its commercial airport, giving the control zone a wide birth. I didn't like the idea of checking in with the control tower every time I turned around, so occasionally, it called for a little tree hopping to avoid being picked up on radar. After this bit of maneuvering, we ended up landing on Lake Charlie, situated approximately six miles northwest of Fort St. John.

ALASKA BOUND

There was supposed to be a seaplane base near the south end of the lake, but all I could see, was one lonely gas pump at a dock I pulled up to. Things sure looked deserted. No one was around to help us, but I did find a note tacked on the wall of a small shack beside the dock. It read, "help yourself to gas and leave your name and address." This guy, whoever he was, was a trusting soul. I had thoughts of having another hassle getting gas.

While we had the opportunity, we refueled the seaplane and checked it over to make sure everything was okay for our departure the following morning. I wrote a thank you note for whomever at the seabase, knowing full well it would be two months or so before I would be back to pay the bill.

We were hungry, and in need of transportation into town. But for the first time, we had the privilege of walking two miles on the Alaskan Highway to a truck stop, where we hesitantly paid a dear price for a hamburger and coke. Luckily, we managed a ride to Fort St. John by one of the locals.

As we approached town, a huge archway over the highway welcomed us to Fort St. John, British Columbia, and the gateway to the Alaska Highway. It had been a long day of flying, and the comforts of a motel would be much to our liking. Myself, as well as Belford and Joyce were quite taken in with the beauty and cleanliness of Fort St. John and its surroundings. Even more so, we were impressed with the smartly dressed Royal Canadian Mounted Police.

This was one night we were going to sleep in a first rate motel. We couldn't have had it better. It did-

ALASKA BOUND

n't take us long to get settled into a room and get cleaned up, out the door again and headed for a restaurant.

We were given directions to a lower level of the building where we entered a very spacious dining room. It was a welcomed change to be practicing a little etiquette in such a beautiful environment.

While enjoying the first real full course meal of the trip, we were highly impressed when twelve or fourteen Mounted Police paraded by us to sit down for supper. They were a sharp looking bunch of men. So well groomed, their hair so neatly trimmed, and boots polished liked a mirror. It was an added treat that helped make a most welcomed reception to British Columbia.

Joyce seemed to be in her glory with all the attractions. She was adjusting to the trip very well. Indian Totem poles decorated the town and stores boasting with souvenirs for the tourists. Everyone took advantage of the conveniences at the motel, while I studied the maps for what lie ahead on the next days flight.

It was the morning of the sixth day. We had flown a total distance of some three thousand miles since leaving home. Looking out of the motel window at seven A.M., we were pleased to be blessed with a clear, sunny day, and not a cloud in the sky. Fortunately, we were given a ride back to the seaplane by one of the employees at the motel.

What hopefully was to be an early start, turned out to be one of those unexpected delays. The night before, I had filled the fuel tanks in the wings chucked full and found the breather pipes still dripping fuel.

ALASKA BOUND

There was a dead calm over the area. Not the slightest breeze was blowing that early in the morning. The lake was so smooth and shiny, it was like a mirror. With these conditions, we would need every bit of help we could get for takeoff, as the altitude of the lake was twenty-six hundred and eighty feet above sea level. This was very high for takeoff with such a big load.

Extra precautions were taken in checking out the seaplane, mainly due to the mountainous terrain we had to fly over on the next leg of the trip. After an unsuccessful attempt to raise anyone at the seabase, we prepared for takeoff. I had a gut feeling we were in for big trouble trying to take off with these kind of conditions with the heavy load we were carrying. Even the little extra gas I squeezed in would help hurt our takeoff. The floats were riding very low in the water, giving another indication of too much weight for the conditions.

There was little choice, but to tempt a takeoff. I tried several times, using all the lake, but the suction created by the glassy water just would not let us break loose. I had seen before, when a mere fifty pounds prevented me from taking off with similar conditions. Then again, the slightest little breeze made all the world of difference.

Frustration set in, as the sun got hotter and higher in the sky. We were losing valuable flying time if we planned to make it to the Alaskan border by night. I shut down the engine to give it a chance to cool off while I proceeded to pump every ounce of water out of the floats. I even went so far as to stepping out onto the floats to relieve myself of any excess weight.

Being so desperate, I begrudgingly emptied out some of the spare gas, hoping that would do the trick. Finally, with the seaplane at the farthest corner of the lake, I pushed the throttle all the way to the dash and preyed we would get in the air.

More weight had to be up front, so I had Belford and Joyce leaned forward to the point where their heads were touching the windshield. We plowed our way down the ten mile lake, trying my best to get the seaplane on the step. Ahead of us, and to my surprise and delight, I noticed a small rough patch of water where a slight breeze had kicked up.

I aimed the seaplane directly for it, and at the moment we got to it, with a little luck and working of the controls, just that smallest amount of lift from the breeze allowed me to get the seaplane onto the step. After that, it was a case of having enough distance left on the lake before I hauled back on the controls to pop the seaplane into the air and clear the trees. With a big sigh of relief from all three of us, we wiped the sweat from our foreheads to sit back and relax, glad to be in the air and on our way.

Following the Alaskan Highway was an experience in itself. We flew over the truck stop we had visited the night before, but this time we were not interested in stopping by for a hamburger. I was wondering why the seaplane was flying so sluggish while climbing. I glanced at the altimeter to see it indicating six thousand feet. We were only a few hundred feet above the highway. We could see travelers of all kinds and shapes scattered along the road. Motor

ALASKA BOUND

homes, campers, truckers, you name it. One thing for sure, I had my eyes glued to the flight map, keeping track of every mile we flew. Where possible, I would fly through mountain passes to save time and pick up the highway at some other point.

The scenery was absolutely gorgeous as we flew over glacial lakes with the pretty color of blue green emerald. Snow capped mountains towered high above us as we flew around each bend of a mountain pass, hoping I could put my trust in the maps. We had the feeling we were like a tiny bird invading the mountain peaks that rose to fifteen thousand feet, or so.

Belford certainly kept his time well occupied, busy with his video camera. I guess one could say, we were all struck with total amazement with such fantastic scenery.

As long as the weather stayed nice, we were in good shape. At one point along the way, we spotted a heard of wild horses not far off the Alaskan highway. Doll sheep and goats could be seen grazing on the rim of the mountains. Eagles soaring high in the sky, would occasionally fold back their wings and come dive bombing past us, perhaps checking us out to see what this monster in the sky was.

Streams of white, milky colored water from the melting glaciers above, flowed swiftly down ravines carved deep into the face of the tall, rugged mountains. Wherever we looked, we could see the work of Mother Nature.

The Rocky Mountain range rose majestically all around us as we continued on, in what I truly call, a

ALASKA BOUND

breath taking, exhilarating, and fantastic experience. All my years of dreaming about seeing this country was finally being realized. As we flew from one beautiful view to the next, all we could say was, "will you look at that , will you look at this."

With a bit of manipulating, by flying through some of the mountain passes, either over, or around parts of the great Rocky Mountains, we managed to make it through British Columbia and into the wild Yukon.

We were suppose to have had enough fuel on board to make it into White Horse, but a glance at the fuel gauges suggested we had better be looking for fuel at the nearest available place. Either I had pumped out too much fuel back at Lake Charlie, or we had picked up some fairly strong headwinds, slowing our ground speed somewhat.

Reverting to the map again, there was supposedly a seaplane base at Car Cross, Yukon. There, I could take on a few extra gallons of fuel to safely get us into the town of White Horse, our next regular scheduled stop. It meant going out of our way slightly, but it was better than taking a chance and running out of fuel.

After breaking out of the high mountains, we found ourselves looking down on what I can only describe as a heavenly valley. A green bed of grass decorated with all kinds of wild flowers and occasionally spotted with spruce trees stretched for miles and miles north and south as far as we could see. It seemed to have been put there purposely by Mother Nature to separate the two big mountain ranges.

Many other valleys wound their way around the base of uncountable spruce laden mountains ranging up to eight thousand feet. Almost every valley had lakes with rivers running through them. Some of the lakes were close to one hundred miles in length. After seeing all of this, I could only think, "paradise."

It would be a half hours flight to Car Cross, and Bennett lake. I knew we would have to keep our fingers crossed on this one, as we would be arriving with very little fuel. There would be no deviation whatsoever, or circling to look at something special, other than head in a straight line for Car Cross.

So far, there had not been much luck accompanying this trip. I had to fight for every mile of progress. As we made a pass over the edge of town where Bennett lake joined Windy lake by a short section of river, we looked frantically for some indication of a seaplane base. By now, it was no surprise, that there was none to be found. In either case, we were forced to land. It was understandable, that once again, getting fuel was going to be a problem.

I landed on Bennett lake, which we later heard, had the reputation as being the roughest lake in the Yukon. What's new? Due to the strong current near the mouth of the river, it was safer to park the seaplane further up the shoreline.

Because the lake was so shallow, we were not able to pull the seaplane all the way to the shore. Not only did I have to use two fifty foot lengths of rope to secure the seaplane, we had to slip off our shoes and wade ashore. That didn't set too well with Joyce, but she laughed it off anyway.

We gathered up the four spare gas cans I had stowed away in the seaplane and made our way a-

ALASKA BOUND

long an old abandoned railroad that had been used for hauling gold oar back in the gold rush days.

As we walked along the railroad, we came upon a few old run down cabins with moose antlers hanging on their front porch. I remember noticing a sign hanging from one of the cabins that read, "Cooper's cabin, Trapper, prospector." These camps probably could have told us quite a story if they could have talked, but who knows what happened to their owners back in the eighteen hundreds.

The railroad led us across a wooden bridge spanning the river, and straight into Car Cross. We had a difficult time trying to convince Joyce the bridge was safe to cross. She was so frightened when she stepped over the open spaces between the railroad timbers and looked down into the swift flowing river, I had to take her by the hand to help guide her across.

Our first glimpse down main street took us back in time to the eighteen hundreds, during the gold rush days. The only thing different, was the lack of people. On the right, was a fur trading post displaying animal trophies, such as grizzly bears, moose, sheep, and many other types of wild life. Next to that, was one of the old ferry boats used to transport the people into Skagway, Alaska, a distance of sixty five miles. It was up on dry dock receiving major repairs. Other than that, there was just a few buildings scattered along the remainder of the right side of the street, which included one shop.

We entered an old general store on the left side of the street, hoping someone could give us information as to where we might find some aviation fuel.

ALASKA BOUND

There again, its contents and surroundings were that of back in the gold rush days. The shelves were loaded with old get well quick remedy medicines, as well as several choices of liniments for aching joints. Such items as chewing tobacco, spices, or whatever else you may have found in an old general store years ago, were on hand.

It would have been interesting for antique collectors, but gas for the seaplane is what we needed. According to the owner of the store, our only hope was an old abandoned airport about five miles out of town.

Much to our dismay, it appeared there was no one available to offer us transportation. I figured this was going to be a long, tedious walk, especially if I had to carry full fuel cans that great a distance. I thought it best to let Belford and Joyce look the town over while I was gone.

In desperation, with gas cans in hand, I started down main street in search of the airport. Not long after I strolled by the swinging doors of a saloon, a van pulled up beside me. I heard the sweet voice of a female ask, "can I be of help to you? I heard you need gas, I will be glad to drive you to the airport."

I took a quick glance at the gal doing the talking, and I don't have to tell you, she sure looked the part of the saloon she had just come out of. Now, I wasn't one to be making snap judgments on people, and I certainly wasn't going to complain or refuse an offer of help under the circumstances, so... I climbed into her van, only to wonder what I had gotten myself into, this time. I remarked, "what a life saver you are," and thanked her for her concerns and kindness.

ALASKA BOUND

We managed to find the airport, if that is what one wants to call it. One short dirt strip, and a broken down shack was all I could see. There was not a soul to be found anywhere. As a last resort, the saloon gal took me to a small shack on the north end of town where an old fashioned round gas pump stood. Using regular gas in such a high performance engine as my seaplane has, was not to my liking, but when in a situation such as this, there was little choice.

Having some high octane gas left to mix with the regular gas was helpful to keep the power up. In the past, I have been forced to run on straight regular low octane fuel. I found it most difficult to maintain altitude with the heavy loads I so often carried. The engine would overheat, along with a few other uncomfortable things, keeping me on edge most of the time.

I had to pump the automobile gas by turning a handle round and round. But believe me, there were no complaints as long as gas flowed out the end of the hose. Some old character, with a beard down to his knees, stepped out of the shack and held his hand out to collect the money, and off we went.

By the time I got back into town I had been given all kinds of offers. Like, "how about staying around for a few days," or "be sure to stop on the way back." I appreciated the saloon gal's help, but I didn't have the time, nor did I have the desire to get involved beyond that.

After meeting up with Belford and Joyce, they got quite a charge out of listening to my story. The gal from the saloon had absolutely refused to accept any money for helping me. At the moment, about all I could do, was wish her good luck. Time was slipping by, so without any further delay, we headed up the railroad and back to the seaplane.

A young Indian boy and girl came up to us on their way back home from school, curious about the seaplane and asking all kinds of questions. It was worth carrying them to the seaplane and letting them sit in the pilot's seat just to see their big happy smile. I bet they won't forget that right away.

I don't know if the few residents of Car Cross were happy to see us leave, but moments later, we were making a pass over the town, waving the seaplane's wings to say good-bye. We then headed north up the valley, which extended all the way to White Horse. An hour later, found us checking in with the White Horse control tower. The seaplane base was inside the control zone, close to town, and I didn't want to invite trouble with the authorities by not checking in.

With clearance to land, we landed just above a dam on the river that flows through White Horse. Power lines crisscrossed the area where hills rose sharply from the river's edge. At the seaplane base, I was surprised to hear we had to wait only twenty minutes for the return of its operator to refuel the seaplane. We took advantage of the break to grab something quick to eat as well as give the seaplane a quick inspection. It was unusual for us not to have problems getting fuel.

Anxious to get on our way, we wasted little time leaving White Horse. The control tower insisted I file a flight plan for the next leg of the trip that would take us to Northway, Alaska. They would notify the U.S.

ALASKA BOUND

Customs of the estimated time of arrival.

There was no getting around this one. They had me over a barrel, so I had to comply. I needed to clear customs on the American border, and it appeared they were not letting me out of their sight unless I filed a flight plan. I can't say, it has been one of my favorite things to be under the wings of a flight plan. At times, it is such a hassle trying to make radio contact with a flight service to let them know you can't make it through because of bad weather, or whatever.

Flying the valleys and low land the rest of the way to the Alaska border was pretty much routine. As we passed over one big lake after the other, snow capped mountains off to our west kept us company most of the way. Outfitters camps could be seen on some of the remote lakes, usually accompanied with a seaplane at their docks.

It was a good feeling to know we were finally arriving at the Alaskan border after flying close to four thousand miles. The control tower at Northway had received my flight plan from White Horse and we were given instructions to land on a lake next to a camp ground south of the airport. They informed us that a Customs agent would meet us, and also have someone bring us fuel for the seaplane. Just sit tight.

Quite some time had passed before the U.S. Customs agent showed up. He arrived in an old beat up pickup truck with the guy that brought my fuel. We were being entertained with some of the campers, so didn't mind the delay. The Customs agent took a quick glance in the direction of the seaplane, asked us a few questions and held out his hand for thirty five dollars. Pretty good pay for not doing much. But then, the guy that brought the fuel charged me six dollars a gallon and added a thirty five dollar bill on top of that for transportation. The total cost of that one stop cost us about three hundred and twenty five dollars. Though I shouldn't complain, I began to wonder if they had some sort of racket going on. What would we have done without their services? I figured this was Alaska. Take it, or leave it.

The one thing I made sure of, was the safety of the seaplane, to secure it to the lakeshore and lock it. The campers at the camp ground agreed to keep an eye on it for the night.

We had hoped to hitch a ride to a motel with the U.S. Customs agent and the guy that owned the truck, but whatever the reason, they refused to take us. They said they would send someone to pick us up. It wasn't long before we heard the sound of squealing tires. Our transportation had just arrived. When I saw the driver stumble out of his car to introduce himself, I shuddered to think of what was to come.

The smell of alcohol was staggering in itself. As we hung on for dear life during a ninety mile an hour ride, my mind flashed back to our experience at Nipawin and our friend Mr. Mitchell, the Robert Redford look alike. While keeping our fingers crossed, we gave each other a questioning look, with the hopes the motel would be just around the corner. But instead, it turned out to be about thirty miles down the road. Worst of all, we pulled up to what looked like a saloon dated back in the eighteen hundreds, during

ALASKA BOUND

the gold rush days.

It seemed we couldn't get away from these sort of situations. If this was supposed to be the comfortable motel we had in mind, we were soon to be in for a big disappointment. As far as I was concerned, I didn't trust the driver as far as I could throw him. The look on his face gave us an uneasy feeling, as though he might be up to something underhanded. Though leery, it appeared we had to play this one out.

We made our way down a narrow corridor into a poorly lighted smoke filled bar room to inquire about accommodations. As my eyes adjusted to the darkness, a most uncomfortable feeling came over me. I noticed several curious onlookers in the back of the saloon peering at us through squinting eyes, checking us out from head to toe. An eerie feeling no less, to be in the midst of such strange company. It made me wonder if these characters were just biding their time for the right moment to slit our throat and make off with our money.

The gal at the bar was fumbling around for a key to a room on the second floor, but she might just as well have hung on to it. When we made a quick inspection of the room, we found the door-lock broken and the door-panel kicked in. The beds sagged worse than an old swayback mare, and there was little privacy between us. The only bathroom was down the hallway which had to be shared by other so-called guests. Being so late at night, it was hopeless to think we could do anything different.

Resigned to our predicament, we set about trying to get a bite to eat. The owner of the establishment was on the verge of a nervous breakdown. Her husband had taken off for White Horse, in the Yukon on a drunken binge and left her with a few screaming brats dropped off by their relatives.

They were breaking everything in sight they could get their hands on, driving her nuts. The restaurant was closed, but among all the confusion, I managed to convince her to cook up some food while I worked on her broken washing machine.

Sometimes, being a bush pilot doesn't mean your job is always flying. There seems to be plenty of other things that go along with the profession. Incidentally, a while back, their right hand man had set fire to the place and disappeared with most of their money and other valuables.

We were quickly finding out, people weren't coming up from the lower states, to Alaska, just for its beauty. Unfortunately, as it turned out, I was unable to fix the washing machine for lack of parts. "Oh well, at least I tried.

The gal that owned the saloon just happened to be a very attractive person. She pleaded for me to take her out of there on my way back through. She was almost hysterical, saying, "I just can't take this kind of life any longer." Probably her husband's drinking and running off on her had something to do with that decision.

The last I spoke with her before retiring, she asked. "Will you fly a circle or two over the saloon when you come back through, I will meet you at the lake by the camp ground?" I know she entered the date on her calendar. Though I thought it best not to

ALASKA BOUND

commit myself, I must admit, the thought of rescuing the fair maiden from her misery, did occur to me. It would be a long time before I forget this stop.

Early the following morning, three anxious people tip-toed quietly down the rickety stairway of the old saloon and out the door, quite relieved to have their money intact and a shirt on their back. We managed to round up a ride back to the lake where our camper friends had kept watch over the seaplane.

The weather had been holding pretty good the last few days, with only a small storm here and there. It was my hope, that this day would be no exception, as Anchorage, Alaska would be our next destination. There would be long stretches of mostly dry waste land, with very few lakes large enough to land on in case of bad weather, or some other unforeseen reason.

After a close check of the seaplane, and pumping out what water there might be in the floats, we proceeded to take off. To keep flight control happy, I felt compelled to file a flight plan with the Northway control tower, clearing me to Anchorage.

We flew the valley following the Tanana River due west for one hundred and fifty miles to Delta Junction. Off in the distance, we could see a large glacier inching its way down from peaked snow capped mountains. Brown streaks of dirt striped the river of ice as it snaked its way through the lower valleys. At the end of the glacier the ice stood several hundred feet high, forming a mass of ice crystals as it finally came to the point of breaking up. Then, to melt and flow freely across the flats of silt and sand to help form a beautiful blue green emerald lake.

As we continued on, capturing the breathtaking view on film with Belford's video camera, I wondered what sort of future lay in store for the distraught lady back in Northway. Knowing how desolate and unforgiving this northern territory is, along with the severe winters, I can well imagine how tough it must be to survive here, especially, without a descent partner.

About an hour out of Anchorage, trouble was staring us right in the face. Black, heavy clouds hung low over the mountain pass which we had to fly through. We had gotten into a bad snow squall. Wet, heavy snow began collecting on the leading edge of the wings, causing some concern, as too much build-up, could cause us to crash.

Because of the high mountains surrounding us, radio contact with flight service at Anchorage was out of the question. We were forced to fly at tree top level, diving in and around the fog as it moved about playing games with us. Certain areas of the pass were much too narrow to do a one eighty, and worse yet, the seaplane was too low on fuel to make it back to the safety of a lake. I had to keep one eye on my flying, and the other on my map to make sure I would not accidentally fly into a dead end mountain pass like so many others have. It would be fatal, to make a mistake here.

Just when things looked next to impossible to continue, the fog would shift, opening a path ahead of us so we could get around the next bend. This was not the same as flying in my own back yard where everything was familiar. Not knowing the terrain, plus the company of the bad weather, sure kept me on my toes. The narrow mountain pass definitely presented a dangerous situation with the presence of rain and snow. Huge glaciers, with their sheer high walls of ragged ice, rose directly under the seaplane's wing tips as we flew low over the end of their long journey down through the mountains.

As each minute ticked by, it brought one more sigh of relief as we found our way through the mountain pass to break out into a large valley overlooking the eastern end of Cook Inlet. Anchorage was only a short flight away, but due to bad weather, we were forced to land at a lake in Palmer. There seemed to be a seaplane of one shape or other, tucked safely away in most every cove. I sought the refuge of an available cove, and called it a day.

We had done well to make it through the mountains, and now, it was time to get something to eat and rest our weary bodies. I am sure Belford and Joyce felt relieved, "after their thrilling ride," to be standing on solid ground. The one thing I had to do in a hurry, was to notify Anchorage flight service by telephone to cancel my flight plan.

Overlooking the lake, was a beautiful restaurant owned by a gentleman retired from employment on the Alaska pipeline. Hanging on the wall of the dining room was a beautiful display of trophy fish and wild game mounts, reminding us, we had arrived in a sportsman's paradise. It was only after a long and interesting conversation about life in Alaska, and its gold mining, that we were able to sit down and relax to enjoy a well prepared steak dinner. The friendli-

ALASKA BOUND

ness and hospitality here, was quite a change, compared to what we had experienced at the old saloon in Northway. The owner of the restaurant was very kind to accommodate us by offering his new motor home for sleeping quarters for the night.

My good friend Bob Hambrecht was in Anchorage, only a phone call away. We were soon in his company, along with his wife, Trudy. While waiting for the weather to clear, we spent the next day visiting. Bob filled us in with all the local news and relative information to do with flying through Lake Clark Pass. It was a shortcut to "No See Um Lodge" where I was to work. We also were given a tour of Anchorage, where several vintage log cabins survived in the surroundings of very modern, up to date buildings.

The latest in shopping stores and hotel accommodations could be found up and down the main thoroughfares. A particular point of interest that caught my eye, was a very attractive information building made of solid logs with a sod roof. It was located in the center of Anchorage and had the most beautiful flowers all around it. A touch of the old times, preserved.

At one o'clock in the morning, we stopped at a picnic area on the outskirts of town to look across Cook Inlet, where we enjoyed seeing a lazy, reddish orange sun hanging in the western horizon. The sun's rays reflected off a mountain named the (Sleeping Lady), lighting up her resting form.

Alaska, is truly a place of beauty. Whatever direction we looked, we were in total awe. The spectacular views of peaked snow capped mountains towering high in the clouds and their many glaciers, left us in disbelief. The clear and beautiful lakes throughout Alaska brought me wishful thoughts of tranquility, as I could picture a comfortable log cabin nestled among northern spruce by the shore. I could see myself sitting back relaxing in a soft easy chair, while proudly looking at my Cessna seaplane (payed in full) pulled up on the beach. How I long for this day.

Adjacent to the Anchorage International Airport, is Lake Hood, the worlds most busiest lake for seaplanes. I was told there was a ten year waiting list for those wanting a permanent parking space for their seaplane. I was lucky to find a place to park for a few hours, and then, the seaplane was in the way of a launching ramp. Because of so much incoming and outgoing traffic, Lake Hood has its own control tower. There was one time, I had to wait more than half an hour just to get clearance to take off.

The next day found the weather on the clearing side of things. After checking with flight service, we packed up our gear and headed for our final destination on the Kvichak River, about two hundred and fifty miles southwest of Anchorage.

As we made our way along the northern shore of Cook Inlet, we flew over an area containing massive barren mud flats. In places, the mud was so deep, it has been known to swallow up man and equipment. It has mostly been created by the movement of glaciers as they plowed and scraped their way through mountains, scooping up soil along their paths. Geese, and other wild fowl attract many sportsman to these very treacherous mud flats where unexpected sucker holes would act like giant vacuums to its victims.

Off to our right, and looking northerly, we could see the breathtaking and magnificent view of Mt. McKinley. Its snow capped peak, at an altitude of twenty thousand, three hundred and twenty feet loomed high above its neighboring mountains. We continued along the northern shore of Cook Inlet and over sloping hillsides, where wide trails and trampled ground around scrub brush showed signs of an abundance of the brown grizzly bear. As we flew over several of these monstrous animals, it only brought to mind how aware we should be, while out in the countryside.

As we entered the mouth of Lake Clark Pass, the safety of the wide open valley soon ended. Sharp, steep, rugged mountain sides narrowed to only a slit through the mountains. Low hanging fog blocked the pass as I tempted to clear some of the higher hills. While listening to other pilots conversing on their radios trying to make it through the pass, a call to flight service on the radio confirmed my fears.

The weather had moved in again, closing the pass to all aircraft and forcing us to change our course of flight. It seemed there was little choice, if we were to get to "No See Um lodge" on the Kvichak River, but to turn back and fly down Cook Inlet towards the Pacific ocean to Mt. St. Augustine, a volcano that towered up out of the Inlet. Thanks to the floats on the seaplane, I could land just about anywhere, that is, with certain exceptions.

We had to fly through the fog, over and under it, and when we arrived at Mt. St. Augustine, I had to fly

ALASKA BOUND

between the steep rocky cliffs of mountain passes, to eventually make it onto Lake Illiamna where Lake Clark Pass makes its way into. I have one or two old sayings relating to my bush flying. "I don't care how close I have to fly to the tops of the trees, as long as I can see what's in front of me." Another, that has long since gone by, "Live dangerously, die young and have a good looking corpse."

Lake Illiamna is about eighty miles in length and supports several outfitters, including an Eskimo village at the southern end where the Kvichak River originates. It is well known for its salmon fishing, rainbow trout and other species of sport fishing. As we flew low over the Eskimo village, we could not help notice the many strings of salmon hung out to dry to aid in their winter supply of food.

Flying further downstream, we passed over sand bars that lay in wait to trap any boat that might venture their way. Other than an occasional stretch of rapids, it seemed wherever there was a small pond, there was a family of swan. It was quite a sight, compared to what we were used to seeing in New Hampshire.

Not long after, we came across a mother grizzly bear with four cubs rolling around on the side hill. We had a ringside seat from the air. We could see the playful action of the cubs as they jumped and crawled over their mother as she lay peacefully, undisturbed by man. She hardly lifted an eyebrow to see what was flying over them.

"No-See-Um Lodge" was approximately fifty miles down the Kvichak River from Lake Illiamna. We had been following the river and flying low so we could watch for wildlife. As we rounded a bend where the water had slowed somewhat, we could see an old barge sitting well upon the shore, listing quite heavily on one side. Unknown to me at the moment, it was to be my home for the next month and a half or so. In back of the barge at the top of the bank, was a newly constructed cedar lodge. Apparently, I had reached my destination, "No-See-Um Lodge," at last.

I pulled the seaplane up to the floating dock near the barge and soon found the three of us in full conversation with the owner, happy to see we had finally arrived. The dock was designed to go up and down because of the tidewater backing upstream from Bristol Bay, part of the Pacific ocean.

Surrounded by miles of open tundra and overlooking the river, stood an older building used to house the owner, his wife, and their helper. A small log cabin nearby presented the only sauna bath within miles. The newly constructed cedar home was to be used by the guests. I was instructed that my sleeping quarters were to be that of the old barge that gave the appearance it might disappear any moment into the fast moving river with the next surge of tide. The cabin floor was sloped so much, I had to block up one end of the bunk about twelve inches to get it level. Pictures on the walls hung precariously out several inches at their bottom.

During the first night on the barge, Belford, Joyce, and I experienced a few stirring moments from the sound of creaks and groans when the barge occasionally shifted. Not wanting to lose my old standby

ALASKA BOUND

Savage rifle I brought with me in case we encountered problems with grizzly bears, I kept it close at hand in case we had to jump clear of the barge.

The next two days were spent doing final preparations for the guests soon to arrive, and giving everyone a chance to get acquainted. At meal time, I soon found out my being a teetotaler, was to pose a problem as far as my eating habits were concerned. I wasn't going to be enjoying the food as much as the others. It seemed that almost all of the cooking included the use of liquor, wine, or beer. There was one cake so heavy with liquor, I swear I could have squeezed a whole cup from it. It was going to be tough to deal with. I could see me being hungry most of the time.

Before the guests arrived and I got too busy flying, the time had come for me to take Belford and Joyce back to Anchorage. Belford had done a lot of filming of the lodge and the surrounding area in his short stay to add to his memories.

My employer hesitantly bid us farewell, wondering if I would make it back in time to fly to King Salmon the following day to pick up his guests arriving by commercial air.

Bad weather threatened our trip into Anchorage. A low dark overcast hung over the area, making it tough flying as we approached the mountains south of Lake Illiamna once again. A white, deadly fog seemed to hide every avenue we wish to take.

There was little chance of us getting through Lake Clark Pass, nor could we sneak through the hills as we had done a few days prior. We found the visibility

ALASKA BOUND

better, by flying near ground level through the low valleys headed for Bruin Pass.

It was tough flying, having to fight our way around thick fog patches at the foot of the mountains, never knowing for sure what we had to face next. At times, we flew so low, some of the grizzly bears we passed over could have stood up on their hind feet and ripped a wing off with one swipe of their giant paws. I am sure it was frightening for both Belford and Joyce, even though they had total trust in my flying. Cautiously, I piloted the seaplane through the valley of Bruin Pass to the waters of Cook Inlet.

Strong winds raked the waters of Cook Inlet, causing huge white caps, creating a dangerous situation. The only sanctuary for a safe landing place may have been in one of the few quiet coves carved out of the cliffs bordering the shoreline. A glance at the altimeter showed we were flying at only twenty five feet above sea level. With the fog riding at the top of the windshield, I had no choice but to keep going, hoping to break into better conditions closer to Anchorage.

Just as we were thinking how alone we were in these crazy conditions, and out in the middle of nowhere, a twin engine land airplane coming from the direction of Kenai, south of Anchorage, passed directly in front of us, headed right for the rocky cliffs. As it disappeared in the fog, I could only "think," this was Alaska, and anything goes when it comes to getting to where you want to go. This was all part of bush flying. I never did hear if the guy in the twin made it, or not.

We had flown more than a hundred miles at water

ALASKA BOUND

level in a game of tag with the spray from the white caps. Finally, the fog gave way to blue sky. Anchorage was just ahead. Belford and Joyce was to spend several weeks with friends of ours, Bob and Trudy Hambrecht, who would act as tour guides for them. They also would have the opportunity to do a little gold prospecting.

Lake Hood was as busy as ever, but fortunately, Bob had made arrangements for an overnight parking space for the seaplane, as we all had been invited to stay at Bob and Trudy's house. While taking in the town and enjoying the sights, I had my last good meal for awhile. I had to leave early in the morning to fly to Wasilla on the north side of Cook Inlet to pick up a young fellow that was to work at the lodge. It was a pleasure to have traveled with Belford and Joyce, and I make mention his generous sharing of expenses throughout our trip from New Hampshire. Joyce has earned her wings. She was ready for another adventure of flying, well prepared to take on all challenges. Belford had collected a diary of his trip on film.

The long flight from Wasilla back to "No-See-Um Lodge" was of the utmost beauty. The weather was clear, with only a few scattered white puffy clouds in the sky. As we passed through the narrow canyon of Lake Clark Pass, I took the opportunity to photograph through the cockpit window the great inspiring view of mighty rivers of ice slowly making their way down from the high mountain peaks to the lower valleys. Glaciers, created from the great depths of snow high on the mountain peaks, crept through every crevasse. Sheer walls of ice glistened brightly from the morning

ALASKA BOUND

sun, while milky white water tumbled its way down rocky steeps into the valley of Lake Clark Pass.

We were amazed to see the perfect reflection of my seaplane on the mirror smooth blue green emerald colored water below us. It could only be described as nothing short of a miraculous and wonderful sight. For forty miles, we could see rugged snow capped mountains ranging up from the shores of Lake Clark. Occasionally, a huge gorge would appear where a finger of the lake would seek sanctuary. Surely, Lake Clark Pass has to be one of Mother Nature's wondrous creations. Outfitters dominated the west end of the lake, giving the sportsmen plenty of good fishing in the available rivers and rapids in the Lake Clark and Lake Illiamna area.

Back at the lodge on the Kvichak River, John welcomed us with a big smile. The look in his eyes told me he had been quite concerned about the bad weather the day before and how happy he was to have a well experienced bush pilot work for him.

It wasn't long before I was into the full swing of things. John had me flying to King Salmon, a small village thirty minutes southwest of the lodge, to pick up guests and supplies arriving by commercial jet. I would fly certain guests assigned to me on daily trips to various chosen salmon rivers, and be their guide as well. The owner, John Holman, would fly four fishermen in his Cessna 185, and I, another four in my Cessna 206 to previous designated hot spots. The hard scrapping king salmon were just starting their run up the rivers to spawn where they had been hatched several years past. Salmon would come by

ALASKA BOUND

the thousands from the depths of the ocean where they spent most of their adult life, to occasionally grow to a weight in excess of a hundred pounds.

Fishermen would stand on the river's edge, casting out their bait or flies, to win or lose in an hour long battle to land one of these big fish. Several times a huge salmon would come along and strip our reels clean of two to three hundred yards of line in its struggle for freedom. Their shiny silver bodies flashing in the sun when leaping from the water while trying to shake free from the hook, only to land with the loud sound "whack" similar to that of a beaver's tail whacking the surface of the water in warning.

We enjoyed these moments of excitement many times, as well as the challenges that went along with it. This repeated itself throughout the ensuing weeks. As new guests arrived, I came to know many new friends. Each fishing excursion usually brought new experiences, including a new adventure.

One thing for sure, I kept my thirty five millimeter camera busy. Capturing the events of the day, as moose or caribou moved along the tundra, or someone wanting to show off their trophy salmon. At lunch time, hot coals from an open fire by the riverside, cooked up a delicious meal of mouth watering pink salmon meat, with a dab of spices, lemon juice and butter. But, when Mr. Grizzly bear happened to come by, he usually would end up with our well prepared meal. Everyone cautiously stepped back to a safe distance while they watched him devour all.

On one occasion, my passengers asked me to fly lower so they could film a giant grizzly we spotted rambling over the tundra. I naturally was quick to o-blige, so made a steep diving turn, taking us only a few feet above the bears head. The bear didn't take too kindly to our face to face meeting. He stood up on his hind feet to challenge this strange looking creature.

From out of the side cockpit window, I looked straight into his fiery eyes as his giant jaws opened wide, showing his bone crushing teeth. Hair stood out on his ruffled neck, warning us to keep our distance. The rough and scraggly fur with dark brown patches told me this was an ugly bear, compared to others I had seen.

As I looked around the cockpit, I could see the expression of fright and relief on the faces of my passengers when I pulled up sharply before the grizzly could reach up with his huge paws. They later told me. "We didn't intend for you to go quite so close to him."

Grizzly bears pose a great danger in the North Country. They have been known to rip through the walls of log cabins just to get a little sugar that got left on a table close to a wall where it can be detected by their keen sense of smell. Stories are told of bears ripping doors off of pickup trucks having groceries left in them. Tail sections of seaplanes, or their floats have been ripped apart because of fish being packed away there. Most outfitters will carry firearms while out fishing to protect their people from such attacks.

One particular day, I flew clients to Katmai National Park to fish for rainbow trout and sockeye salmon. A doctor, his son and their wives thought they might

ALASKA BOUND

like an easy, relaxing day for a change. As we made our way along the river, walking in a grizzly trail that most people thought to be man made, we noticed several grizzlies upstream. They were busy attacking the salmon in the middle of their spawning run. I had told my clients to keep an eye out in case the bears moved onto our side of the river.

The next turn in the trail brought us face to face with one of the grizzlies. He was only twenty five feet away. When he reared up on his hind feet, my four friends started screaming and ran back down the trail. I managed to bring their quick exit to a halt and calm them down a bit, while explaining to them, that was the worst thing they could do. That sort of action only frustrates a bear, and could only bring more problems. Only after things had calmed down, and the grizzly and I had time enough to check each other out, did he finally drop down on all fours and slowly circle around us to disappear down the river.

After that little episode, we proceeded more cautiously to a waterfall, popular for both humans and grizzly bears. A team of Japanese photographers had installed a remote controlled underwater camera at the base of the waterfall to capture the scene of thousands of salmon and the activity of the bears chasing them back and forth for a healthy meal. As the salmon made their desperate leap up the waterfall, some of the not so fortunate were dazed when striking the rocks and would fall prey to the bears and eagles waiting below.

We stood on a grated platform overlooking the river that gave us little sense of security. It was apparent the bears were more interested in the salmon than us. It was quite an experience to see the bears jumping around the waterfalls catching fish in mid air, either with their jaws, or their clawed feet.

Bald eagles grabbed their share of fish. While they ate their catch in the quiet of the trampled grass on the edge of the river, magpies pecked away at their feathers, trying to distract them so they could have their fair share of the catch. No fisherman in his right mind would dare carry a sandwich or candy bar, for fear a bear would get a whiff of it and wind up missing half his clothes, or an arm or two.

When the action on the river slowed, and most of the bears had lumbered out of sight to digest their gorging of fish, we decided to pack up our cameras and head back towards the seaplane. We chose a different route that led us through a heavily wooded area on a path crisscrossed with grizzly trails. I had gotten a glimpse of a bear, but figured it best to keep it to myself. I didn't want another catastrophe on my hands.

No sooner had we stepped out on a road leading back towards the seaplane, when the doctor said. "Richard, I saw something big and brown moving towards us in the woods from where we just came." The moment I saw what he was talking about, for their safety, I sent the four of them down the road several hundred feet.

Moments later, as I readied my camera, the grand daddy of all the grizzly bears in the Katmai National Park and his female companion stepped into the road only a few feet from me. I stood frozen in my tracks, not wanting to cause any excitement while taking pictures of the huge male bear frothing at the mouth, trying to make out with his friend. She would spin around and viciously strike him with powerful blows to the head during his persistent actions. The two great animals reared up on their hind feet and battled furiously, flailing out with their gigantic paws.

They were too involved to notice me standing close by. This was a once in a lifetime opportunity to capture on film. But to my great disappointment, I soon realized the film was slipping on the advance mechanism, so all my efforts were for naught. I had no further opportunity to correct things, as a park ranger vehicle rounded the bend, driving the bears into the woods.

The doctor and family were quite taken in with what they had witnessed on this day, as it was far from their planned day of relaxation.

At the mouth of the river where I parked my seaplane, the water was teaming with red salmon. Everyone enjoyed the fishing tremendously, more than one could imagine.

Later in the day, while relaxing on the bank of the river, we watched three fishermen run for their lives out into the lake. They had several fish laying at their feet, when two grizzlies making their way down the river, suddenly stopped, stood straight up on their hind feet, and pointed their nose straight towards the fishermen. It wasn't long before they got wind of the fish. All the men could do, was to stand at bay, waist high in the lake, and watch the two bear devour their fish.

ALASKA BOUND

This all got to be common experiences throughout my stay while working for "No-See-Um Lodge," flying around the tundra and crystal clear lakes in the mountains. At one of those clear lakes, I had the surprise of my life when I reached down with a canoe paddle to push the seaplane back to shore. Thinking the water was only two feet deep or so, I lunged with the paddle, but instead, it was nearer ten feet deep. I found the paddle a little too short and almost went head first into the lake.

At the lodge, a new group of fishermen out of Thunder Bay, Ontario were busy tending the gill nets they had strung out in the river. They were complaining, that something was eating the sockeye salmon caught in the net, and they couldn't figure what. I later pointed out a bald eagle as being the culprit. It was standing in the river with his feet locked on top of the net while he stuck his head underwater to rip chunks of fish away with his beak.

Another day, an eagle was seen lying flat out in the river with its wings stretched out, giving one the appearance it was drowning. The fast current was carrying it downstream at a steady pace, so our brave sportsmen set off anxiously by boat to its rescue. I laughed as they followed the eagle to shore, watching it flapping his giant wings and hopping into a small tree.

Back at the dock, proudly praising themselves of rescuing the eagle, they were surprised to see the eagle back in the river, doing the very same thing again. It was one of the ways an eagle fishes. By laying flat in the water with his head under the surface,

ALASKA BOUND

he can watch the salmon as they swim by and grab one for his meal.

My two months stay in Alaska had fulfilled my long time dreams. I had survived all kinds of challenges to come here, and now it was time to leave. The memories will be with me forever of those I flew and guided throughout the Bristol Bay area in western Alaska, the Katmai National Park, and Tic Chic Lakes region. I also learned of a monopoly some Eskimos have delivering supplies and equipment to many of the outfitters along the different rivers.

My experiences were far too many to mention all of them. But one thing is certain, Alaska with all its magnificence, is truly a sportsman's paradise, loaded with adventure. I leave behind its majestic beauty of peaked snow capped mountains rising high in the sky and the slow moving glacial wonders that have hidden history for thousands of years past. The beautiful blue green emerald lakes and green hillsides laden with the many varieties of wild flowers.

To top it off, I make mention the discovery of a rich lode of gold in the hills near one of those crystal clear lakes I had flown to for arctic char fishing. My statement that day, "I'll bet there's gold in them thar hills," was truer than I thought. Too bad I didn't find it.

As I bid farewell, the land of the midnight sun held true to its name.